NEVER GIVE UP!

Riding the Emotional Rollercoaster of an Autism Parent

by Monique Cain

Published by 3MT Media 2019

Copyright © 2019 by Monique Cain

TheEverydayAutismSeries.com.au

A catalogue record for this book is available from the National Library of Australia.

Book cover design by Purpose Group
Illustrations by Andrew Louis
Typesetting and e-book formatting services by SelfPublishingLab.com

ISBN:
978-0-6483461-2-8 (pbk)
978-0-6483461-3-5 (e-bk)

For More Resources and Support on coping with autism and educating friends and family head to:

TheEverydayAutismSeries.com.au/resources

For regular inspiration and encouragement or to learn more about our autism journey go to:

Facebook.com/theeverydayautismseries
Instagram.com/theeverydayautismseries

To purchase *The Everyday Autism Series* picture books go to:

TheEverydayAutismSeries.com.au/books

Contents

Foreword

"When you've met one person with autism,
you've met one person with autism."
~ Dr. Stephen Shore

I speak frequently at seminars on autism. I spend a lot of time talking to parents whose children are on the spectrum. I live every day with two autistic children, and I know the challenges and the joys that brings. Maybe I've looked into your eyes and told you that it's going to be OK... no matter what your child can and cannot do, through all the hopes and the heartaches, the impossible decisions and the uncertainties, they'll still be your child and you will survive. Maybe we'll never meet in person... and this book is the only time you'll hear my voice: Whatever your situation, I want to say, "Never give up!"

This is not a textbook on autism. I don't have any qualifications in special education, neuroscience, or any other related professional field to back up my advice although I've talked to more specialists than I can keep track of. However, it is my hope and belief that it will encourage parents whose children have been diagnosed with ASD and who are on the roller coaster of emotion and experience that come with the diagnosis and the suspicions that led to that diagnosis. I've tried to be honest. I never want to sugar-coat the pain that comes with parenting a child on the autism spectrum, or the challenges, or the tears… I know that some parents have a much more difficult time than we have had, and that we are only in the early stages of the journey. But I also know it's easy to focus on the difficulties and to ignore the rays of sunshine.

I hope you'll find encouragement, truth, and hope in these pages. When you're parenting a child with autism it's especially important to take each day as it comes and to soak up the small successes as they come. Perhaps other parents wouldn't see much to rejoice about, but you know how much that tiny smile, the whispered words of thanks, the fleeting moment of eye contact means.

You can read this book from start to finish. You can dip into individual chapters that interest you. The chapters are deliberately short. I know that when you have children on the autism spectrum you can't count on long periods of quiet to read and it's great to be able to actually finish a section, so you create a sense of momentum and progress for yourself.

I'd love to hear from you one day.

Dedication

This book is dedicated to my family and to all the other families affected by, and living with, autism.

I hope that telling my story can give you valuable insight, knowledge and inspiration to never give up on your child, your life, or your hope.

PART ONE

Our Journey-
Encouragement

"I thought I would have to teach my
child about the world, it turns out I have
to teach the world about my child."

~ HIPPOQUOTES.COM

Introduction

A Letter to My Babies

"The most important thing to me now
is that my kids are happy and that
they know that they are loved."

~ Monique Cain

To my two beautiful children, in particular my daughter Madi, I'm so sorry I didn't completely understand what was going on in the beginning, but now I know more...

We have all been on this autism journey together as a family, living, and learning. Along the way the two of you have taught me the true definition of unconditional love... and I don't just mean that you have taught me to love each of you for who you are, I'm also talking about the unconditional love you have shown to me when I was unable to understand your struggles. I've also learned that love doesn't need words to express itself truly.

I have learned...

- New meanings and deeper levels of patience from you and I thank you for being patient with me, too.
- To keep trying, no matter what happens and never give up... because you haven't failed until you quit.

3

- To appreciate all the little things in life and to recognise what is most important to us.
- To be more kind, caring, compassionate, understanding and open to other people, things, and ideas.
- To withhold judgement... because I cannot see inside another person's heart and mind.

I have become a better person because you came into my life.

I am so proud of the beautiful souls you are and the people you are growing to be. You are both leaving a very special mark and lasting impression on every single person you meet.

I will continue to do everything in my power to make your lives as happy and comfortable as I can. I love you both, you bring me so much joy and insight. So often, when I am encouraging you to persevere, to step out of your comfort zone, to be patient... I am speaking to myself as well and taking courage from **your** example.

You are my absolute inspiration! I am so proud of you and hope that you are proud of yourselves too. I love you both more than words can say.

Chapter One

High Hopes and Shattered Dreams...

"I casually thought I could write a book about my life one day, but I never thought that my story would be anything like this!"

~ MONIQUE CAIN

Everyone has an idea of what life will be like once you become a parent. You imagine your child hitting each of the growth and development milestones on time, showing their particular areas of interest and excellence. You think about the sort of mother you will be, the experiences you will share with your children, and the life you will have together.

Unfortunately, things don't always go according to your plan. Sometimes, life throws you a massive curve ball and the life you imagined veers off in new directions that are completely out of your control. That's what happened to my husband and I when both of our children, Madi and Thomas, were diagnosed with Autism Spectrum Disorder (ASD). In light of this diagnosis, to say that the last six years of our lives have been an emotional rollercoaster would be an understatement.

A Fairy Tale Romance

My husband and I met during high school. We got together at a weekend party when we were just sixteen and seventeen years old. After our first kiss, I knew I had found someone very special. I never spoke to my parents about boys I was interested in, but that night I went home and told them that I'd met someone. I said, "You'd really like him Dad, he's good at football." I went on to say, "I could marry this guy!" I'd clearly had a bit too much to drink and was on cloud nine. Little did we know it at the time, but that is exactly what happened…

After a few bumps in the relationship and a break when I travelled overseas, we decided to get back together and commit to each other for good. Before I even arrived home, we had bought a block of land. So, my future husband picked me up from the airport and we began to plant some seeds for our future at the ages of twenty-four and twenty-five. We had our whole lives ahead of us and we were looking forward to every moment!

I had always wondered, "How could you possibly find your soul mate in your little home town, when there's a whole big world out there?" Well, it turns out that you don't need to search the whole world. Sometimes they're right there beside you.

Michael clearly was my soul mate, my equal. The person that loved me no matter what, just because I was me. We could do anything together: go for a run, have a drink, watch a movie, have fun, talk or be quiet together. We simply enjoyed each other's company. He made me want to be a better person and I had the same effect on him. Our unwritten plan was to eventually get married and have a family. I had always wanted kids and one of the main reasons I wanted to marry Michael was because I knew, without a doubt, that he would be an extraordinary father.

And Then There Was More...

So, I was engaged to be married to my high school sweetheart, the love of my life. Our wedding date was set, and I had just celebrated my twenty-eighth birthday when I unexpectedly fell pregnant with our daughter Madi. Stubborn and strong minded even in the womb, she was uncompromisingly breech, so she was born by caesarian section in February 2009. For the first eighteen months she seemed to be developing well, making animal noises, counting to 10, and recognizing colours. However, by her second birthday, Madi was not talking at all, was not interested in playing with other kids, and she had no interest in opening her birthday presents... I thought this was a bit strange, but since Madi was our first child, I didn't know what to expect. I had also just found out I was a few weeks pregnant with our son, Thomas so I had other things to think about.

As time went on, Madi started displaying more unusual behaviours. I was worried by her obsession with lining things up, her social isolation and her unwillingness to make eye contact. Despite the reassurances of our friends and family who said that she was fine, and that all children develop at their own rate, Michael and I felt uneasy.

When Madi's behaviour continued to become more worrying, we sought professional help. So, when she was three and Thomas was just four months, Madi was diagnosed with ASD.

So, there I was, a four-month-old baby and a three-year-old with a diagnosis of full-blown Autism Spectrum Disorder (which I didn't really understand, but which terrified me). It felt like the end of the world... and in a way it was... the end of the fantasy world that I'd always imagined.

Chapter Two

A Terrifying Diagnosis...

"Life is... not about counting the losses
and the lost expectations, but rather
swimming, with as much grace as can
be mustered, in the joy of all of it,"

~ LEISA HAMMETT

I remember the day Michael, Madi, and I walked into the speech therapist's office for the initial diagnosis appointment. A few minutes into the session, before doing any formal assessment she said bluntly, "Yes, she definitely has autism." Everything that went on after that is just a blur.

After the appointment, we sat in our car in the car park and we both broke down completely and bawled our eyes out. We were terrified. There was something seriously wrong with our little girl and we had no idea what that really meant or how to fix her.

Once we had this diagnosis, our pediatrician said that Madi would need between thirty and forty hours per week of therapy to have any chance of further development. Thirty to forty hours per week! We knew something wasn't right, but we had never imagined it would be such a severe problem.

When we told our family and friends about the outcome of our assessment and what had just transpired, I felt they were still in denial. They were all very reassuring, saying things like, "She's fine, there's nothing wrong with her." Or, "She'll be fine, you'll all be fine."

With all our hearts we wanted them to be right, but we knew they weren't. Yes, kids do learn and progress at different times, but in the back of my mind I knew this wasn't just a child operating on her own schedule. The professional's verdict had confirmed that uneasy gut feeling that I'm sure every parent experiences… the one you need to trust even when you don't like what it is saying to you.

I'm Not Even Sure What Autism Is...

Even today there are a lot of myths about autism and an incredible amount of ignorance in the general population. I know that in the midst of our initial shock at the diagnosis we felt a huge wave of fear of the unknown… fear that the professionals we saw didn't exactly dispel.

It's not that long since children who were not 'normal' in every way were automatically placed into Special Schools. Certainly, if there were any children on the autism spectrum at my own school, they must have been very mild cases or very well disguised. To me, the phrase 'Autism Spectrum Disorder' conjured up someone who was visibly different, so how could that possibly be a correct diagnosis for our beautiful, blue-eyed Madi?

We Didn't Know Then... But We Were Ready to Learn

Sometimes, the shock of a reality that is worse than you ever imagined it could be sets you on a new path. As we sat out there in the car park bawling our eyes out, Michael and I decided that we were going to do everything we could to give Madi all the help she needed to grow and thrive, autistic or not. I was clearly going to need to take charge of learning everything I possibly could about autism, and I was going to be busy taking Madi to appointments, working with her at home, and taking care of baby Thomas... and yes, we were both wondering whether Thomas would be autistic too.

Never Give Up... Because You Don't Know the End!

The pediatrician definitely told us that Autism Spectrum Disorder was a whole range of symptoms with different degrees of severity and that it was too early to tell what Madi would eventually be capable of. I don't think we really heard him. Even if we did, I'm not sure that we really understood how much that message mattered... then.

Today, I want every parent to hear that message loud and clear! If I had that knowledge in front of me, on some of those days when everything went wrong and I felt like a failure as a wife, as a mother, as a person, I might not have despaired so much. No-one knows what any child – especially any autistic child - will ultimately be capable of... or how much joy they will bring along the way. Be open to the everyday joys and successes, treasure the insights you receive along the way... and don't give up, no matter how dark your path seems.

Chapter Three

What Signs Did We See?

"What's going on in that beautiful mind?"

~ John Legend

Looking back now, there were definitely early signs of autism long before we started to think something was wrong, but at the time we didn't recognise them for what they were or understand what they meant. We were first-time parents, and like all first-timers, we received a lot of advice. Some of it conflicting. Even our family and close-friends were confident that it was our parenting style that was the problem, and we were told on the one hand that, "She needs to be shown more discipline;" and on the other that, "She needs to be shown more affection." It's not like we didn't try but it was easier said than done...

Obsessive Behaviours

All kids like repetition and predictability, but Madi was truly obsessive about this. She would watch the same DVD, over and over again for hours on end. *High 5* was a perennial favourite. In the playground, Madi would want to be continually pushed on the swing for at least an hour at a time. It became such a repetitive

occurrence that I actually made up a song/poem type story while
standing there pushing her...

Swing, swing, swing, swing
Swinging through the air;
Up and back, up and back
Swinging without a care.

Swing, swing, swing, swing
Swinging through the air;
Up and back, up and back
Higher if you dare.

Higher Madi, Higher Madi
So high you touch the sky;
Higher Madi, higher Madi
So high that you can fly.

Higher Madi, higher Madi
Higher hold on tight,
Fly Madi, Fly Madi
To the sky till day turns night.

Swing, swing, swing, swing
Swinging threw the air;
Up and back, up and back
Swinging without a care.

~ MONIQUE CAIN

13

Lining things up in carefully ordered rows was one of the more obvious obsessive traits, but Madi loved to do this with unusual objects. She would get all the sauces and bottles out of the fridge and line them up on the kitchen bench.

Food & Other Sensory Aversions

Madi was an easy baby to feed, but suddenly her diet changed dramatically. She went from eating pretty much everything to being extremely fussy about food. There were times that I was afraid she would starve it was so difficult to find things she would eat.

Trying to get her dressed was a nightmare. She couldn't tell us what she was feeling, but it was clear that putting on clothes made her skin crawl and she acted as though we were torturing her. We bought so many clothes and shoes that she never wore or used, and people used to stare at us with judgement in their eyes when they saw her running around with summer clothes and no shoes when it was freezing cold outside. Forget about pretty headbands, beautiful bows, or cute little ponytails. Even from a very young age, she hated anything in her hair... I was lucky if she would even let me brush it.

She stopped having a nap during the day and didn't want to go to sleep till really late at night and she was still waking up early too, so I thought maybe she was over-tired... or strong minded like her mum and wanting control of her own life.

Creative Play and Communication

We noticed fairly early that Madi wasn't showing any of the normal signs of creative play. She didn't play with dolls, dress-ups or any of her toys, yet she would play for hours at a time on her own outside with a leaf, a blade of grass, or a puddle. For her this was totally absorbing entertainment. We wasted so much money on toys she never used!

Other mums had stories about the funny words and silly sayings their kids came out with. My child wasn't speaking at all, she didn't even say, "Mum," and sometimes when my friends would complain laughingly that their children never stopped talking my stomach would tighten and I'd have to swallow the cry that wanted to come out, "Treasure those words, every single one! You don't know how lucky you are." It's not that I wanted their children not to speak, it's just that when you don't know if your own child will **ever** say anything, you recognise how precious every word is. You see, Madi couldn't tell me if she felt sick, what she liked or didn't like, and I thought that I might never hear her speaking voice at all. Watching a tiny toddler, much younger than Madi having full-on conversations was, and still is, very hard to swallow.

Another tell-tale sign was that Madi did not make eye contact with anyone. We couldn't look into her eyes and feel as though we were making a real connection and it was devastating. She would look away or ignore us completely.

Sometimes we wondered if she had a problem with her hearing. Talking to her could be like talking to a brick wall. After asking her twenty times to do something, I would get so frustrated because

15

she wasn't responding and raise my voice, not understanding what was really going on. It felt as though she was deliberately ignoring us, especially one time when she was playing with a blade of grass for about an hour, just totally fixated on it. We needed to get into the car to go somewhere and she simply did not respond.

Going to public events, like family fun days where there were many people was a monumental ordeal. Madi didn't understand that she had to wait in line for her turn on a ride and we couldn't make her do so. She thought it was like the swings in the park that went on and on until she was ready to stop.

Chapter Four

Dealing with Diagnosis

"Autism is not a disability,
It's a different ability."

~ Stuart Duncan

I am not a professional therapist or psychologist and I don't pretend to be one, but my husband and I have lived and breathed autism every minute of every day for the last seven years with both of our children on the spectrum. We have been exposed to many different scenarios and felt every raw emotion... the highs as well as the devastating lows.

You have a vision of how your life will be when you have kids, what they will be like, what they will be good at, and what you will be able to do or achieve as a family. So, when all your hopes and dreams are crushed and the reality of an autism diagnosis sets in, it can feel quite soul-destroying. Looking back, I can say that I had to be broken down in order to be re-modelled into a more humane person. At the time it just felt as though I was being torn apart... beyond any hope of repair.

It takes time to come to terms with a diagnosis like this, even though autism is not a death sentence. You go through a kind of grieving process: grieving the loss of the child you thought they would become and the life you thought you would have. When Madi was diagnosed, we didn't know what ASD really meant, so there was also a journey of discovery that took us into some pretty dark places. When Thomas started to display some of the early warning signs we had experienced with Madi, we imagined the whole process starting again. We really didn't want to believe our instincts. We wanted to trust the friends and family members who said, "He's just copying his big sister." But by then we knew the importance of early intervention and we trusted our feelings, rather than the tantalising voice that promised, "It couldn't possibly happen to you twice!"

Was the diagnosis easier to cope with the second time? No, it definitely was not!

We had more information. We had more experience, but it was like finally putting to bed our hopes of ever having a 'happy family'. We didn't yet know that there are moments of intense sweetness in the midst of this journey... as our children reach milestones we never expected they could. We were terrified of where this journey would take us.

With both of my children diagnosed with ASD I was heading down a road to a dark place. I was still working, I was taking the kids to all their necessary therapies and appointments, they were fed and cared for, but I was suffering in silence. I couldn't talk to anyone about the kids without breaking down, so I began to withdraw. Most nights I'd cry myself to sleep. I was drinking too much, too often, and I was desperately unhappy.

Seeking Help and Taking Responsibility for Self-Care

Finally, after reaching rock-bottom, I decided I didn't want to be unhappy anymore, for the sake of myself, my husband, and my kids. I was very kindly offered some counselling sessions which initially I refused. Looking back, this was a major turning point! The first few sessions, I pretty much cried the whole time, but I needed to. My counsellor reassured me that it was completely normal and OK to feel the way I was feeling and have my thoughts about the whole situation. She also encouraged me to write, which has been an amazing form of therapy for me. Through the therapy and what I have learned at seminars I have realised the importance of taking care of my own needs and happiness. This is not selfishness (as I used to think), it's an important way of helping my children thrive.

I don't think it is a coincidence that since my happiness and my mental health have improved, my children have made significant progress as well and I think this is really important to emphasise. People with autism (especially children) are unusually sensitive to the atmosphere and energy around them. This is one of the reasons why it is so difficult for them to be surrounded by groups or crowds: the onslaught of conflicting emotions confuses and overwhelms them. Therefore, when I do everything in my control to truly be the most positive, happy version of me that I can be, my kids respond to this very well.

What I have discovered is that when I am in a positive frame of mind, have a more optimistic approach and outlook, a better acceptance of how our life is, and who our kids are everything

19

runs smoothly. We obviously still have our moments, and those moments can be terrible at times, but I can truly say we are much happier and more open to appreciating the truly joyous moments when they arise.

All you can do is your best on any given day, considering how you feel and what you are facing. I try to take things day by day, not thinking too far ahead. The kids are constantly surprising us. When I was trying to plan ahead and focusing on what wasn't right, trying to be a perfect parent, and not taking care of myself, I would miss those moments of joyful celebration. Now we are better able to respond in the moment, to love our children dearly, and be proud of the happy, unique, beautiful souls they are rather than beating ourselves up over what they are not!

Chapter Five

Out and About - Social & Personal Pressure

"I got to a point where I didn't want to leave
the house because it was all just too hard."
~ MONIQUE CAIN

After seven years, I'm still not completely sure that I will ever be 100 per cent OK, but then I look around at others and ask, "What does OK look like, anyway?" The truth is that every day is a mental battle and there is no escaping our reality which is a need to be ready for whatever that day may present.

Strangers Who Judge

Once upon a time, I was probably one of those people: judging other parents on the basis of what I could see on the surface. I don't remember if I did make snap judgements, I certainly never said anything aloud to other parents, but I know better now.

Outings like going to the supermarket were an absolute nightmare! Madi would run away from me, which was seriously stressful because she couldn't talk to anyone if she got lost. She couldn't respond to a question or even tell anyone her name. As a lot of kids do, she must have thought it was a fun game to run and hide between and behind clothes racks, but one day I actually lost her. I was pregnant with Thomas and I had no idea what to do! I searched high and low and asked random people in the store if they had seen a little girl by herself. They probably thought I was a totally negligent mother as I had to think hard about what she was wearing (they didn't know about the struggle we had had to get her dressed at all)! Totally embarrassed and seriously scared, I approached a staff member and asked if they would help me look for her. They broadcast a message over the PA and, soon after, a gentleman brought her back to the shop. She had actually left that area and headed into the central part of the shopping centre. I can't express the terrible feeling of fear, panic, and self-condemnation I felt, and Madi was totally oblivious to it. Thank God an honest man brought her back to me!

I tried to keep Madi confined and entertained in trolleys but was conscious of judgmental looks and condemnatory stares when people saw a girl who was 'far too old' to be sitting in the trolley. It was a 'damned if you do, damned if you don't' situation: if she was in the trolley, I was a bad parent, if she was roaming free and running away from me or grabbing things off the shelves, I was a bad parent. These were total strangers, but somehow what they thought about my parenting mattered to me.

After Thomas was born, it got worse! One day, I was going through the checkout, with baby Thomas in the capsule part of the trolley and a very irritable Madi in the other part. She was making such a fuss that I reluctantly let her out and instantly, she was off. I had to decide very quickly what to do. My groceries were on the conveyer belt, my baby and handbag in the trolley, people were waiting behind me in the queue, but I felt that I had no other choice but to leave everything and run after her.

Once Thomas grew older and had similar reactions and behaviours, taking both of them with me became increasingly difficult. Strangers would stare, give me judgemental looks and make disparaging comments which did not help my mental and emotional state at all, especially when my children were already challenging me. It seemed as though every time we set foot near a shop something dramatic and stressful would occur. My anticipation of a disaster didn't help either. If I had to take them to the supermarket, I would have them both confined in the trolley, bribed and distracted by food. I would then steel myself to ignore the strangers who would say things to me like, "They're too big to be in a trolley." or "Isn't she cold?" because my daughter wasn't wearing a jumper. Why can't people just mind their own business and keep their opinions to themselves? More often than not, after one of these excursions I would end up sitting in my car crying after a 'quick trip to the supermarket'.

I got to the point where I would drive half an hour to my parents' house so they could mind the kids while I went shopping. Occasionally, I would also drop them off with my husband at work or pick him up so he could wait with them in the car while I quickly ran in to get a few things (and I know that I was very lucky to have that option).

Friends and Family

We certainly got more well-meaning advice than we could ever use from our friends and family, but there were also the comments that hurt just because our parenting experience was so different. It's not that we begrudged our friends and family members' happy experiences, it's just that they made us feel as though we're aliens.

When catching up with friends, they would all discuss how they wish their children would stop talking and go to sleep, while I'd be sitting there in silence, praying that my child would say just one word. Going to a kinder concert, I would watch while all the other kids were singing songs and doing the actions while my child is having a meltdown in front of everyone. Celebrating the achievements of my friends' kids and trying to ignore their pitying looks has always been hard to handle.

Birthdays, Christmas, and other special occasions were extremely stressful and not fun at all because the kids had no comprehension of what was really going on. I would be on tenterhooks hoping they wouldn't offend anyone and that no-one would mention the fact that Madi's hair wasn't brushed or that neither child was wearing shoes even if it was the middle of winter.

Self Judgement

It can be very isolating being an autism parent. After you've experienced so much obvious disapproval every time you go out, you start to expect it. Maybe sometimes I saw condemnation when it wasn't there, but most of the time it was unmistakeable. I lost count of the number of times I received uninvited and hurtful critical comments about my children and my parenting skills from strangers, but I can count on the fingers of one hand the times I received encouragement and kindness from them.

Every time my kids misbehaved, I was also judging myself. I always felt the need to explain and thought of wearing a t-shirt or even a sign on my head that said, "My child is autistic."

We got to a point where none of us wanted to leave our house or attend any events or occasions because it was either too confronting, or we couldn't face the inevitable incident. It was basically all too hard.

Chapter Six

What Do We Do Now?

"We haven't put all of our eggs in one basket, we tried many different options and have revisited them all at different times..."

~ Monique Cain

We were devastated by both Madi's and Thomas' diagnoses, but we knew we had to set things in place as soon as possible because the one consistent piece of advice we received was that early intervention was critical. Madi's diagnosis was especially overwhelming! We were given a lot of options by our pediatrician but had no idea which ones we should choose. Everywhere we looked for information confused us further and it felt as though the more we learned the less we understood.

Thomas's first year of life was a complete blur. Madi was three and she was attending some sort of appointment or session every day of the week, I was trying to get back to working two days a week. We had just moved into our new home and we had a sense of urgency about finding 'the right interventions' for Madi. Looking back, I wish someone had told me to take a deep breath and trust my judgement, instead I felt an internal pressure to do and try everything that was suggested... to make sure we left no stone unturned in our quest to help our precious daughter.

Every time we went to an appointment we heard about more options. So, we saw more professionals, filled out more forms. Oh, those forms and those initial appointments! The same questions over and over... When did she crawl? When did she walk? How was your pregnancy? Blah, blah, blah. How I hated filling out those forms and answering those questions! All I wanted was someone to help my child... now!

We decided to try bits of everything:

- Speech therapy;
- Government play group sessions with occupational therapists and other special needs kids and their parents;
- Day care and kinder for exposure to mainstream settings and other children her age;
- Special development pre-school to cater for more of her needs...

We were very fortunate that both my husband and I worked in our family business, so we were able to be flexible with our working hours to allow us to make all the running around possible, but still... all those appointments were sucking up our time and money. We were trying to fit in all the homework and exercises to ensure that we were giving Madi every opportunity to make progress.

I lost track of all the things we tried for Madi. We persisted with each of them for a period of time but if we didn't see any progress, we would change things up. We were desperate, and then... we started worrying about Thomas' development, too.

When well-meaning friends and family said things like, "Thomas is fine, he's just copying Madi's behaviour." Or "He's OK, you're just so busy with Madi you don't have as much time to spend with him," it felt as though someone had stuck a knife into my heart. My preoccupation with my precious daughter was costing my son, too! I didn't know if I could cope with the guilt.

I suppose that every parent wonders if they've 'done enough' especially when their children have problems, but what is 'enough'? Whatever it was, I was convinced that I wasn't doing it... but I didn't know what more I could do. Some days I was so overburdened with guilt that it was all I could do to get out of bed. If that sounds familiar, let me tell you that it doesn't end there. What you can do **is** enough!

A Ray of Hope

One of the things that turned our journey around was talking to a client from work who also had a son with Autism. This family was a godsend! They gave us so much necessary information about their journey and the things they had learned. It was so helpful to speak to another Autism parent who had walked the path we were walking. Until then, we didn't personally know anyone else whose kids had Autism and we were still learning about what it involved. I think we were still in a significant state of shock. This family told us how we could go about getting help, the people they were seeing, the different things they had tried, and the places they took their son. They also encouraged us to hope and persevere and introduced us to a one-on-one Applied Behavioural Analysis (ABA) Therapy Centre which they had found extremely effective.

We'd already tried a wide variety of different types of professional help, but we trusted this family's advice and soon started ABA therapy. It truly transformed both our family's and Madi's lives. We finally found all the support, help, and guidance we needed, and it was integrated in a single location. When we started ABA, Madi was non-verbal, unable to sit to complete a task, not toilet trained, and basically trapped in her own world. We needed to start by working on the most basic skills and behaviours before speech or other therapies could be helpful.

We worked on helping her sit at a table and complete a given task, make eye contact, copy a simple movement, or follow a basic instruction. Madi responded so well to the one-on-one, intense, repetitive, exercise and positive reinforcement she received, and it was so carefully designed to meet her particular needs that she made dramatic progress. This made all the intense work worthwhile and we began to talk cautiously about enrolling her in a mainstream kinder.

Chapter Seven

An Unknown Landscape to Explore

To enter the unknown
And live it everyday
Not knowing how to deal with it…
How to feel or what to say.

Crushed by the news of one –
To have your heart broken once more.
To find the energy, the fight, the love
To pick yourself up off the floor.

Fighting demons in my head
Facing people that judge and stare
Not hearing our children's voices
Finding any way not to care

People don't quite understand
The heartache you go through…

Many are caring and sympathetic
They have their own demons too.

Missing all those funny comments
Talking to a brick wall
No sleepovers or cute friendly play dates
No conversation at all.

Seeing a glimpse of hope
After crying lots of tears
Trying to stay positive
Pushing away thoughts of later years

We are always up and down
But we are slowly improving
Things could be always worse
As long as the rollercoaster keeps moving

It has been a real battle so far
What a journey, what things we have seen,
It may never really be over
And we'll never forget where we have been.
~ MONIQUE CAIN

For parents of autistic children every new day, every new stage, is a journey into the unknown. It's like being an explorer or pioneer because you never know what is ahead. Yesterday's

31

achievements may have been a breathtaking triumph, but today could spiral into disaster in the blink of an eye. I learned never to take any achievement for granted... to receive each one as a gift and to work very hard to manage my own fears and expectations.

I mentioned that my counsellor encouraged me to take time to write. The act of exploring and sharing my thoughts and emotions on the blank page without judgement and with as much honesty as I could muster was particularly challenging at first. I found myself thinking, "Oh, you can't write that down. A good mother/wife/person would never think/feel that way!" Sometimes I'd listen to my inner self... other times I'd ignore it and say, "But that's how I am thinking and feeling." I learned that the act of expressing myself honestly and without judgement was an important step in releasing my own self-condemnation. Often it helped me to tease out some insight - into myself, my children, my circumstances - and that enabled me to make decisions as well as to take each day as it comes.

Managing Fear... and Hope!

I suppose every parent wonders what the future will hold for their children, but I think for parents of autistic children that 'wonder' is better translated as 'fear'. I've explored the reality of that further in another chapter. Here, I want to focus on what I, as a parent, see as my responsibility on a daily basis.

Every single day, I have a choice: I can dwell on my fears and hopes and let them shape my thoughts and actions, or I can do the best I can with the landscape I'm faced with. I have found that the days I let my imagination run away with me, whether I'm imagining worst case scenarios or optimistic daydreams are the days we all struggle most. I find it helpful to take each day as it comes, do what is necessary, be grateful for progress, learn from failure, then release it. I don't always make the right choices, but the more often I do, the happier we all are.

My hopes can be just as distracting as my fears. As each milestone is reached, I look to the next one... and experience intense frustration when the path forward gets rocky, or we seem to be heading backwards. That's why I try to process and release each day before I go to bed so that I can start every new day afresh.

Chapter Eight

Focus on Progress

"Parents who have children with
special needs are always thankful
for progress not perfection."
~ A VERY SPECIAL NEEDS RESOURCE

When our friends introduced us to Applied Behavioural Analysis (ABA) Therapy and we started to see Madi make progress we were ecstatic! It was a very long and slow process, step by step (sometimes backwards). As the parent of a child with autism, it's always hard to keep the balance between reality and hope... hope keeps us moving forward, but sometimes it also breaks our spirit when we let our dreams fly ahead of the progress.

ABA helped us to understand our child more and taught us different ways of approaching challenging circumstances. We learned how to teach our child by breaking things down into basic steps and work towards each small goal until we finally achieved the bigger one. We learned to truly celebrate each of those tiny steps and to recognise them for the achievement they are... both for our children and ourselves.

The whole process was emotionally draining but also life changing. Slowly, we were learning to enter into Madi's world, to communicate with her, and help her reach out to communicate with a world that seemed hostile and alien. We were able to unlock doors that a few months earlier we thought would never open.

How Much Courage Does Life Take?

The expectations of parents, teachers, and society in general is based on an 'average' level of sensitivity and responsiveness. I put 'average' in inverted commas because we all know there is no such thing. Neuroscience is only starting to pinpoint the reality of heightened sensitivity to various triggers that is often part of autism and can be responsible for the intolerance of noise, stimulus, crowds etc. but one of our biggest lessons was just how much of daily life batters the senses and emotions of people with autism and the courage and energy required to cope.

First Madi and then Thomas have shown us how people can slowly build up tolerances to things that used to feel unbearably uncomfortable. They have shown us that patient and persistent practice really does change everything. They have learned to be in noisy crowded places and accept the intense discomfort and insecurity that brings. They are learning new skills and coping with changes in routine, and we have also learned to look at everything from a new perspective.

Courage comes in many different forms. The progress our children have made has given us so much hope for a better and brighter future for each of them and our whole family. It has helped us to have a more positive attitude, to aim higher and be more confident in what we all may be able to achieve. As we look back and reflect on all the progress we have seen so far, we know we're looking at a miracle... and so we have reason to hope for even more amazing results as the years pass.

We're Celebrating the Milestones One-by-One

Since we began to get help after Madi's diagnosis, we have seen a very slow but gradual progression with her learning and behaviour. In the early years of intervention there were months (maybe even years) when nothing really seemed to change, but over the last twelve months we've seen her jumping ahead by leaps and bounds. She is tasting new foods, surprising us with unprompted speech and responses, forming friendships, playing creatively, ... sometimes it seems as though we see progress every day.

Thomas is still quite affected by his sensory issues, but his tolerance is increasing. Even when he can't talk to the other kids they often join in his games. I believe that he feels like he is free to be himself, and I have a feeling that both his and Madi's confidence and progress stem from my own acceptance of the challenges we face and my choice to face it with hope and optimism.

Chapter Nine

Trust Your Judgement

"We have been truly blessed to have so many special souls helping us along the way. It has been a monumental team effort!"

~ Monique Cain

No-one else knows your child like you do, even if you are a first-time parent. I know that every parent has moments of anxiety about their child's development and well-being, but, if there's one thing we've learned about autism, it's that the earlier you can start therapy the better your outcomes are likely to be. If you seriously suspect that your child has any degree of autism, then pursuing an evaluation is **not** a waste of time or money. It will bring you peace of mind and it will relieve you of the guilt of thinking, "If only I had followed my instinct and acknowledged something might be wrong!"

Thomas seemed different to Madi. He made eye contact, he wanted attention and interaction, he was walking at nine and a half months... but his speech was not developing. He wasn't meeting the standard requirements for verbal development at our maternal health nurse appointments. At eighteen months he was completely non-verbal, at two he still did not speak, he was not toilet trained, unable to play creatively or complete a given task, and we thought he might be starting to show signs of sensory issues.

At the same time most of our friends and family thought he was fine. The carers at his daycare centre didn't think there were any issues. He was quite different to Madi and the general consensus was that he was just copying some of her behaviour as younger siblings do. Maybe he wasn't talking because Madi didn't talk. Maybe he was just copying her reaction to noise and crowds and clothing.

I just had the same unsettling feeling that something wasn't quite right just as I'd had with Madi. I asked other parents about the siblings of their autistic children and they all said they didn't have any issues and had met all the milestones, so we spoke to the professionals where Madi was going to therapy. They suggested that starting him in therapy early wouldn't hurt if it turned out there was nothing wrong and would be a great help if he did, in fact, have autism.

Although we were not one hundred per cent sure and we fervently hoped that we were wrong, knowing how important early intervention was, we got the ball rolling. Within a few weeks, just after his second birthday, Thomas was also diagnosed with ASD.

In Denial

Human emotions are pretty strange! Michael and I had been suspicious about the behaviour we were seeing and had pushed for this evaluation yet... I was still in denial for a while about Thomas's diagnosis.

I remember being at a fellow autism mum's house, organising a fundraiser for our kids' ABA therapy centre. Her husband was heading off to Bunnings and I joked with him, suggesting he take two autistic kids with him, meaning Madi and their son. He corrected me and said, "No, you mean three." I paused for a moment and thought to myself "Oh, yeh! Maybe?" I still hadn't completely accepted the fact of Thomas's diagnosis.

Madi's difficulties and limitations were more obvious and when people would then ask, "Is Thomas on the spectrum too?" my instinctive response was, "No." It was partly wishful thinking, partly an acknowledgement that he's different from Madi.

No parent wants to put a label on their child, and we all want our children to be talented, successful, and fit in with their peers. Maybe we need to rethink the way we look at 'labels'. In the case of autism, the label is really an acknowledgement that we are looking at a person who is going to struggle to fit in with many aspects of 21st century society, so they need extra help in order to flourish. Autism is a particularly tricky diagnosis because it can look so different in each individual child (and adult!). I think Thomas's diagnosis is a great example of the importance of trusting your own gut feeling:

- We suspected he had a problem.
- At the same time, he was quite different from Madi (and other autistic children we knew).
- We really didn't want to hear that he had a problem (we wanted a "no" diagnosis desperately).

- However, we knew the importance of early intervention if he was on the autism spectrum.
- I am extremely glad that we didn't let our intense desire for everything to be normal, keep us from taking early action.

Hard as the reality of Thomas' diagnosis was, it was far better than pretending everything was OK and finding out later that it wasn't.

Chapter Ten

Professional Help

"I might hit developmental and societal
milestones in a different order than
my peers, but I am able to accomplish
these small victories on my own time."
~ HALEY MOSS

We've worked with a lot of professionals in various areas to help our children reach milestones and overcome challenges. From the time Madi was diagnosed with ASD just before she turned three, she has had a full schedule. Thomas's interventions started when he was two. We have tried just about everything from day care, main stream kinder, one-on-one ABA therapy, speech therapy, group therapy sessions with Occupational Therapists, special development school, dance classes, swimming lessons and park plays. My advice is now to try everything, continue with what works, remember that you can always change what you are doing or try something new, and know that different strategies work for different children.

If there's one thing I've learned from my own experience and from talking with others, it's that there is no single 'right' path.

ASD just isn't that simple and straightforward. We've tried to strike a balance between perseverance and intuition.

Any kind of change is challenging and takes time to adjust and adapt to, especially for kids with ASD. That includes new therapies, places, and activities, and, of course, the kids (and professionals) have good days and bad ones. However, I think you get a sense fairly quickly about most things that you should follow even when the person or therapy comes highly recommended by someone you trust.

We have been so lucky to have been associated with a lot of very special and extremely dedicated professionals along the way who have dramatically helped us with our kids, have touched our lives unforgettably, and left a massive impact and imprint. We are so grateful for each of them, and we will certainly never forget how important they have been. Knowing that your children are in the hands of people who genuinely care for and about them, makes an incredible difference. We've even had people who have told us that they are not (or are no longer) the best choice for our children and we are so grateful for their honesty.

Applied Behavioural Analysis (ABA) Therapy

We'd already seen many therapists of different kinds before our friends introduced us to ABA. For us, that simplified our life and provided us with incredible support during the early stages of our journey. As we faced each new step, issue, or phase, they helped us evaluate options and they supported Madi in every possible way: sending therapists to kinder sessions, helping teachers and other children understand Madi and learn how to interact with her.

We would have been absolutely lost without ABA. The therapists, staff, and other families at the centre became like our extended family. They knew and understood what we were going through, could empathise, advise and help us more than anyone. As we set goals, determined actions, faced setbacks, and celebrated achievements they gave us the strength to survive. It is so comforting to be part of a community of support, when once we had felt so helpless and alone.

Beyond ABA

We've had a fantastic experience with all of the aides that have supported us at kinder and school. There is an amazing Autism community, mostly hidden from sight, full of people who want to help others and they have an incredible depth of compassion, experience, and wisdom. It is such a reassuring feeling and so rewarding to be able to give back to others.

At the same time, don't listen to everyone either. We have chosen to stop various therapies for both Madi and Thomas because we weren't seeing results or because we just had a feeling that it wasn't the right thing to do at that time, even when we didn't have any real evidence. Everyone is different, every child is different, and you'll need to do a lot by trial and error. I recommend that you listen to everyone's advice and decide what works best for you and your child. It's one of those areas where **you** need to take responsibility for your decisions.

When Madi was finishing her second year at kinder (after a great year with a fantastic teacher) we were trying to decide whether to send her to mainstream school. We weren't sure if she would cope and her teacher really didn't think she would cope at all, but she is now in her fourth year and thriving. It was one of those situations where we had to make a judgement call between well-informed, caring, yet conflicting opinions. It feels as though we are constantly defying the odds, proving people wrong, and defying myths. I've got a feeling this is life with autism. Society tends to use a lot of adjectives such as 'normal', 'regular' and 'mainstream' but extraordinary is our 'norm'. We don't know any different.

Chapter Eleven

You Never Know What Will Happen Next

"We know what we are but know
not what we may be."

~ WILLIAM SHAKESPEARE

Friends

Madi has made a friend! One of those things that I thought would never happen. A little girl the same age as Madi (just turned nine) whose birthday is just a few days after Madi's, genuinely wants to be her friend. She likes Madi for who she is Autism and all. They met at school about twelve months ago and their friendship has blossomed and gone from strength to strength since. They play together every play time, have regular play dates after school, and have started a weekly tap dance class together. She gets excited when Madi says something new or responds appropriately to her. They have a special hand shake just between the two of them. She accepts Madi's vigorous cuddles, knows that she may need a break and that play dates may need to be cut short. They enjoy the same activities including drawing, painting, singing, and dancing.

Madi's friend has even written her own version of the Madi story books. She was recently presented with a very special award at school, "Aussie of the month: For helping educate others about autism and for being a wonderful friend that promotes inclusion." We are so grateful to have her in our lives and thankful to the school for recognising her contribution.

Every parent wants their children to have friends. Every child wants a friend who accepts them for who they are... and fears that they will never find a person like that. It has been hard for Madi to form friendships due to the language barrier, but there are and have been a few very special souls who have been attracted to Madi for who she is and have made a major effort to reach out to her. This is one of those circumstances that makes me want to cry and dance in the same moment. It's precious in itself, and if Madi has a friend who loves her just the way she is, who knows what else could happen!

Thomas is an absolute character. He has a very kind, cheeky, fun-loving personality, with an overactive imagination. The stuff he comes out with is hilarious and so damn cute! His creative play is now off the charts. All the girls love him, and lots of kids join in with his adventurous imagination, games, and love for playing chasey. There is a little boy in his grade at school who said that Thomas was his best friend.

Milestones

The best advice I can give to other parents is to never give up! If something is too hard or doesn't work out the first time, try and try again. Whether it's five minutes later, the next day, month, or year, if you give things another go and keep trying you may end up pleasantly surprised. It may take more tries than you hoped for, but you'd be astonished how many things eventually work out.

When Madi was small she wouldn't let me brush her hair and I lost count of the accusing looks I received from strangers at the grocery store when they looked at the tangles in her unbrushed hair. These days, I get so much joy from being able to brush her hair and put it into a ponytail before school even if it is sometimes a mad rush. She doesn't love having her hair brushed, and when she's nervous or tense it even hurts her, but it is still pure joy... a milestone we never thought we'd reach. Something so little and insignificant for others is absolutely huge for us.

After so many years' silence during which my children never spoke, it still absolutely amazes me every day when I hear them speak and I never get tired of hearing their voices. I promised myself that I will never tell them to be quiet after so many years wishing and praying for them to speak, especially that precious word, "Mum." We still can't hold a proper conversation, but I will hold on to that hope and believe that one day it may happen. I know that many families don't yet have that privilege and I am so grateful for all the milestones we have reached even as I dream of reaching farther.

Mainstream School

Both Thomas and Madi are now at mainstream school, with aide assistance and they are doing exceptionally well. The other kids cheer them on and both of them usually participate in the activities.

The assistance of the aides plays a critical role in Thomas and Madi's progress to the next level. They send me photos and video footage nearly every day showing their progress and special moments. Without that evidence, I would hardly believe all the things they can accomplish and I have been able to share those achievements on my social media pages to show other people who are following our journey. Our friends and family are usually quite surprised and excited by what they see too, and it helps other parents, families, teachers, and educators to gain knowledge and hope by seeing all the progress as well as the ways in which they are being included, supported, and encouraged to succeed.

A fellow inspiring local Autism mum has helped pave the way for us at our mainstream school! Her son, who had previously attended our ABA therapy center, was struggling a bit, so she decided to start her own foundation that raises money to fund for the assistance of ABA therapy at our school! Both kids are benefitting from The Light Up Autism Foundation, which provides 1 hour of ABA therapy each day, performed by their trained aides during school hours to assist in all the areas where they need extra help. What an amazing initiative by this mum! Her son has now graduated to secondary school, but she is still continuing to run the foundation to help others! We are so grateful and absolutely blessed to have this option available, especially considering how well our children responded to ABA and how they were already used to that way of learning. Hopefully, in the near future many more schools will offer this option too!

Family

As a family we enjoy swimming, going on walks, parks, riding bikes, scooting, watching movies and visiting grandparents. After everything that has transpired, I honestly could not wish for more and absolutely love the fact that we can enjoy doing all these things together now. We are actually getting to enjoy some of the true joys of parenting because we never gave up.

Chapter Twelve

A Love Song

"We contain the shapes of trees and the movement of rivers and stars within us."

~ PATRICK JASPER LEE

I love both Madi and Thomas so much. They are my babies that grew inside me, my flesh and blood. They both have truly beautiful souls and special gifts and the world would be a poorer place without them. Regardless of our difficulties, I still feel blessed. A lot of people aren't able to conceive or experience the joy of having kids and despite all of our challenges we have been lucky enough to experience that.

People often ask me if the kids play together, if they ever speak to each other, and how they behave towards each other at home. Honestly, I find it really fascinating and quite humbling to watch. They look out for each other and you can tell they genuinely care for each other. If I get angry or raise my voice at one of them, the other becomes defensive and gets upset as well. Even though no words are exchanged their underlying love shines through and demonstrates that love needs no words.

My Name is Madi
And Thomas is my brother
We are a family and will
Always look out for each other.

We love to play outside
Running and jumping together
The beach, the park or sprinkler
Depending on the weather.

We spend hours on the swing
Swinging side by side
We look over at each other
With beaming smiles of pride.

We like to jump and cuddle
On our mum and dad's bed
Watching TV or movies
And sometimes we bump our head.

We always stick together
Especially when mum gets mad
If she raises her voice at one of us
The other gets upset, cries and is sad.

I love my brother Thomas
He is my best friend
Near or far, where ever we are
Our friendship will never end.
~ Monique Cain

Speaking of love raises the question of what we would have done differently if we knew our kids would have to deal with Autism. There's no getting away from the fact that there are questions about how they will cope when my husband and I are no longer there to support them, although we still don't know how far they will come before that day arrives.

We are often asked what we think causes Autism. To me, the cause doesn't actually matter and it's still very difficult to separate myth from science on the subject. It is what it is, and we just have to deal with it in the best way we can. When professionals have suggested that we should have genetic testing done I have been hesitant, partly because for a long time I wasn't ready to hear what the results might say. Even if we had known that our children would have Autism, my husband and I were always going to be together and we were always going to have kids. The only difference is that we might have felt guilty about our decision.

Recently our psychologist suggested we should think seriously about having genetic testing in case we decided to have more kids… or in case one day our kids would like to reproduce! OMG, I could not even imagine that at this stage! That's really thinking a long way ahead, but I guess you never know. We are pretty much reconciled to the fact that we won't be having any more children ourselves, even though we are finally at the point where life is a lot easier. It's hard because I do still think about it, but with two out of two children diagnosed with ASD, I feel that the odds of another child we conceived not having any learning difficulties are slim. I would be completely paranoid about the possibility and throwing another child into our life would change our whole world and its dynamic.

We are trying to put necessary things in place, so the kids are provided for financially whatever happens because their future is still unknown. We are not sure at this stage whether they will be able to hold down jobs. However, if you had asked me a few years ago I would have said, "No way." but now I'm thinking, "Why not?" They have come so far... and we have learned so much. Maybe by the time they are ready to work the world will have changed enough for each of them to be accepted and valued for their contribution no matter what that looks like.

A few years ago, all my dreams had died, now I have thoughts of Madi going from a child who couldn't speak to a contestant on The Voice. Thomas might be a pilot, considering how he loves all things that fly. Who knows what miracles the future will hold? And really, as long as they are happy and loved, I will be happy!

Chapter Thirteen

Separation Anxiety and Rediscovering Joy

"This is a FOREVER journey with this
creative, funny, highly intelligent,
aggressive, impulsive, nonsocial,
behavioral, often times loving individual.
The nurse said to me after 6 hours with
him, 'He is a gift!' INDEED he is!"

~ Janet Frenchette Held

I am sure every parent experiences a form of separation anxiety or guilt when they leave their child for the first time. That feeling is exacerbated when you see your child crying or screaming as you leave or hear the report of their distress.

For me, those feelings escalated when my daughter's behaviour became increasingly more difficult to understand or control. Not being able to verbally communicate, not knowing how much she understood, and seeing her absolutely hysterical every time I left her was heartbreaking. I felt like she was only truly comfortable with my husband or myself so I felt terrible for her sake, but I also knew how difficult she could be and how emotionally draining caring for her could be. I felt guilty shifting that burden onto others, even if only for a few hours.

It seemed as though every new stage carried its own drama! I will never forget her first session of ABA, when I walked away from her room. She was so distraught that she had to be physically restrained from running after me by the trained professionals. One day at kinder, her teacher had to call me to collect her because they had been trying unsuccessfully to re-clothe her for forty minutes in a bathroom. On her first day at school Madi was desperate to escape. It ended up with Madi barricaded in the library with a staff member, and Madi was screaming the 'F' word repeatedly as she tried to escape. These are just a few of the distressing images imprinted on my brain that made me feel guilty for leaving her. As a result, we questioned our decisions even though we thought we were acting in her best interests for the future.

Leaving her with grandparents was also difficult although she gradually became comfortable with them. At first, I would have to stay for a while and wait until she was distracted before I could sneak out, otherwise she would have a major meltdown. The idea of leaving her with friends or a babysitter was just impossible and when Thomas started to exhibit signs of autism leaving our two children with anyone was not an easy thing to accomplish.

Guilt and Reality

When your child cannot communicate verbally and shows their distress tempestuously you don't just feel guilty about leaving them. You also feel guilty about putting the burden of dealing with them onto another person even if it's just for a short time. At the same time, the ongoing stress of your situation makes objective analysis of your own needs almost impossible.

The months and years of feeling helpless in the face of a desperate desire to protect and nurture your child, trapped in a volatile situation, and absolutely heart broken by the possibilities of our children's future, and our own, took their toll. As time passed, rather than becoming accustomed to the drama, I felt worse each time I left the children to go to work on two-days each week and nights out with my husband and friends seemed inexcusable. When I did go out, I felt so guilty that I didn't enjoy myself. The next day would be even worse. In addition to holding on to the guilt from the night before, the hangover from alcohol heightened all those feelings of depression which were constantly with me.

Learning to Let Go

One of the key learnings I gained from my own counselling sessions was the importance of taking care of myself and confronting my emotions rather than trying to hide from them. It has taken years to overcome those feelings of guilt and the compulsion to suppress my own needs and, of course, because the kids have dramatically improved, it is now easier to leave them. However, I wish I had given myself permission to have fun when I did leave them much sooner.

I didn't keep count of the number of nights when we planned everything, steeled ourselves to leave the kids despite their distress, and went out but could not let go and actually have fun and enjoy ourselves. I am quite sure that this not only deprived us of much-needed relaxation, but also deprived our kids of the refreshed and energised mother who could have helped them more.

Life was not fun and as much as you try, you can't fake it all the time. The stress spills over. I don't beat myself up over that anymore (at least not usually), but I believe that one of the greatest gifts we can give our families (especially when we are under constant stress) is a sense of presence. Both the good and the bad moments **will pass**. They don't last forever so I try to be especially present in those joyful moments of celebration and relaxation… they are my source of energy for the next crisis.

I didn't learn to do this all at once. It's a constant choice, of course, but sharing (and crying) during counselling and my daily practice of writing about how I am really feeling has made a tremendous difference.

Recently, I was honoured to be invited to be a bridesmaid for one of my oldest and dearest friends. For her hen's celebration we went away for a whole weekend. I can honestly say, that not once did I feel guilty about my decision when I thought about them at home. I laughed, let loose, and had one of the best weekends of all time… and when I got back home the kids were totally fine, and happy to see their relaxed and happy mum.

Chapter Fourteen

Madi's Dance Through Life

"For autistic individuals to succeed in this
world, they need to find their strengths and
the people that will help them get to their
hopes and dreams. In order to do so,
the ability to make and keep friends is
a must. Amongst those friends, there
must be mentors to show them the way.
A supportive environment where they can
learn from their mistakes is what we as
a society needs to create for them."

~ BILL WONG, AUTISTIC OCCUPATIONAL THERAPIST

From the moment I gave birth to my little girl, I was so excited to think of all the girly things and activities she was going to do and all the special things we would be able to do together. I started dancing at three years old and have been teaching dance for over 10 years. I just naturally thought that my daughter Madi would be a dancer too, and could not wait to see her under lights, in costume, on stage.

Madi seemed to really enjoy moving to music right from the start. She was obsessed with *The Wiggles* and *High 5* and would copy actions and follow movements from the television, so I started taking her to dance classes at around the age of two years old.

In the beginning she seemed to cope OK. She joined in with pieces of the class, and as she was still very young we kept persevering with it. However, as she got older, she started to regress and become more isolated and consumed in her own world and things like following the steps of a dance routine, participating in a class, or wearing the appropriate clothing, especially costumes, would turn out to be almost impossible. Once she was diagnosed with ASD all the different therapies, sessions and appointments took over our lives and dancing took a back seat.

Madi still seemed to really enjoy music and dancing and research shows that it is a really good form of learning and therapy, especially for kids with ASD so each year we would make another attempt to bring her to dance classes. Unfortunately, she didn't have the attention span and it was way too distracting for all the other kids to have Madi in their class. We would persist for four or five classes at the beginning of each year, but it just wasn't working and was too emotionally draining and stressful for both of us, I ended up in tears after nearly every class.

When Madi was eight, my dance teacher and I decided to try a special all-abilities dance class for Madi and other kids with additional needs. We created a modified class in which kids were free to wear whatever clothing they were comfortable in, provided specific dots and spots to guide their movements, played quieter music, used dimmer lighting, and made the classes shorter with a smaller number of students, more basic steps and routines: overall a more comfortable environment in which the kids could find the freedom to enjoy dance and music. This has been a great gift to Madi and other special needs kids as well as their parents.

As a parent in this environment I don't have to feel uncomfortable, embarrassed, or worried that my child is behaving badly or distracting the other kids. Instead, my child is able to enjoy as much or as little of the class as she can cope with and reap the benefits of music and dancing as well as exploring a new way of self-expression.

Madi has continued to thrive at dance classes! By the third term she was participating for the duration of the class, following the routines, and she even managed to perform at the end of year concert. I don't think there was a dry eye in the house. Everyone there knew the journey it has been to get to this point.

I always knew that dancing was something that she really liked and that it would be good for her, it just took time, patience, and some extra thought to unlock her love for it. Along the way, I sometimes asked myself if I was encouraging her dancing for myself or for her. I can honestly answer that when you have a sense that something will help you need to trust your instincts and persevere... trying, trying, and trying again, modifying your approach until you succeed.

One week at dancing, Madi was sitting on her teacher's lap after class (an achievement in itself!) when she said, unprompted, "I love you, Sheron!" One of those absolutely heart melting-moments, none of us will ever forget and a tribute to another important person in her life, who persisted and never gave up!

Every Mother's Dream

From the moment you were born
I had huge hopes and dreams
To be best friends, mother and daughter
For you to wear my jeans

To dress you up in pretty dresses
Paint nails and do your hair
Put make up on, be girly girls
Be happy and for you to care

I hoped you'd be good at dancing
At netball and at school
Be a model or a movie star
Be popular and cool

I hoped we could have conversations
And get to talk about boys
That you can enjoy great friendships
A family and all the joys

I know that you are special
Beautiful inside and out
Extremely smart and talented
I am so lucky, without a doubt

As I look into your eyes
I wonder what you are thinking?
I wish you could tell me everything
To stop my heart from sinking

You don't have to be like me
You will find your own way
You are an amazing individual
And that is more than okay

I love you and I'm so proud
And just want what's best for you
I hope that you know how much
And love me and are proud too

~ **MONIQUE CAIN**

Chapter Fifteen

Family Support Was My Lifeline...
What is Yours?

"Parents have therapists come in their
house and tell them what to do. They
give their power away. Parents need
to focus on healing and empowering
themselves. They must shift their beliefs
about autism. Once the parent knows
who they are the child will respond."

~ LORI SHAYEV

We were extremely fortunate. Both our parents live nearby, and they were available to help us. I know that not everyone has this privilege. Our parents became our best friends. Apart from our own home, their houses were our safe haven. It took some time before our kids were comfortable in their grandparents' homes, but they were the first people with whom I felt comfortable or confident to leave my children. Madi and Thomas are the only two grandchildren on both sides of our families, so they are very much loved, and it definitely helped that both sets of parents are still together, so they could always manage two kids by having one each.

They are the perfect illustration of how your children grow up, but are always in your care. As we went through the upheaval of diagnosis and therapy while dealing with the stresses and strains of daily life, our parents were always there for us to lean on when we needed a break. Our life at that time was really hard and extremely emotional.

Feeling Outcast

As our children grew up, we realised how different our family life was to that of other families. This made it hard to get together with the mums in my mothers' group, old friends, or other mums at school. Play dates were rare (and often ended in tears), sleep-overs non-existent, and children's parties a disaster. The kids' concerts, as well as parents' or grandparent's nights at kinder were excruciatingly painful. Our children did not want to join in with any of the activities, or participate in the group songs, dancing, or actions. Instead, they were either attempting to escape, hiding behind us, or sitting on the floor playing by themselves. We were agitated and embarrassed and either felt or imagined the pitying looks that were being cast at us.

Even special family occasions like Christmas and birthdays were devastating. At Christmas there was no huge build up or excitement leading up to the day. No requests for presents, letters to Santa, or desire for reassurance that they hadn't been naughty. We didn't put out cookies, milk, or carrots for the reindeer. The anticipation, joy, and excitement were all absent from our lives.

Unexpected Lessons

It has taught us a lot
To appreciate all the little things
To put things in perspective
And enjoy what loving children brings

It helps to talk to people
Going through the same pain
You are not alone in this
Knowledge and comfort, you will gain

We have had heaps of support
To help us learn and get through
From our parents, friends and professionals
We didn't know what to do?

We will never give up
And we won't stop fighting for
Our children's future or happiness
Nothing else means more.
~ MONIQUE CAIN

You Need Various Sources of Support

While I recognise how fortunate we are in our family support, we also have other sources of support which are equally available to all parents of autistic children. No matter how independent and self-sufficient you are, this is not a situation you want to deal with by yourself and it's important to have other people in your life whom you and your children can trust.

Some places you can find support include:

Other ASD Parents: Don't be afraid to speak to other ASD parents and ask their opinions and advice. Although it can be very emotional and every situation is different, they can relate to most of the things you are going through and have probably experienced similar scenarios. It helps to feel that you are not alone and to talk to someone who knows how hard life can be. I have also found that many (but not all) of the autism support groups are great sources of ideas, encouragement, and practical help. Getting involved with these is also a great way of paying forward all the help that you received.

Trained Professionals: Sometimes you need a trained professional to turn for advice and assistance and these can be very helpful. I've already talked about how much ABA helped our children… and that's not just a question of their professional expertise, but also their desire to help both our children and us. However, not all professional advice is created equal, so it's up to you to sift through it and determine what fits in with your family needs and values.

Over the years, and still to a certain degree now, we have had a lot of issues with sleeping arrangements and the kids wanting to co-sleep with us. I still can hardly believe the pediatrician who told us that the only way that we could rectify that situation was to put a lock on the outside of our daughter's bedroom door! I did not even consider that option for one second, but apparently it is quite common advice.

It is still rare for my husband and I to have an uninterrupted night's sleep. There were nights where Madi was awake for two, three, four, or even five hours at a time, nearly seven days a week. This went on for at least eighteen months. Once she commenced therapy, group sessions, and appointments every day of the week, our sleepless nights were far less frequent.

Educators: We have encountered some of the most amazingly dedicated teachers and aides in our local kinder, primary school, and dance studio! They may not have the specific training to deal with special needs kids but their enthusiasm and desire to help makes up for it. It's especially encouraging when you think that most parents are also not special needs trained but we still do a great job.

Seminars: I used to avoid seminars, partly because it was hard to organise logistically, but every time I have attended one, I have brought away some gems of advice or information that made it very worthwhile. At an "I Can" seminar a couple of years ago they talked about support networks and enabling. Two things really resonated with me and affected the choices I made: The first thing is to make sure your child has a good support network in addition to their parents both in case of emergency and as extra support and perspective. We are so lucky to have both sets of grandparents, but our kids also have had caring and invested therapists and aides along the way and we try to provide a network of reliable and special people in their lives. The second thing I learned was to encourage your child's loves and interests regardless of how strange or left field they may seem. For Thomas this has been providing him space for his paper crafts and imaginative play while Madi has had her singing and dancing.

When our kids were first diagnosed, I couldn't bring myself to read a lot of helpful information or attend any sort of presentations. I recognise that I may not have been ready mentally and emotionally to find comfort in those settings, but in hindsight I'd encourage others to push themselves in this area if it is at all possible.

These days I try to attend as many seminars as I can. I always gain valuable knowledge. Even if I have heard similar information before, it is a good refresher and reassures me that we are on the right track and doing the best that we can.

Chapter Sixteen

Focus on the Good and Avoid Comparisons

"When you focus on the good,
the good gets better."
~ ABRAHAM HICKS

Over the last few years, we have been faced with many mentally challenging situations. It is hard to constantly pick yourself up, keep a straight face, and not automatically respond with a negative comment or comparison. We have learnt to appreciate the little things in life and do our best to keep everything in perspective. We make a consistent effort to focus on things that are truly important in life, especially in relation to our family and make a conscious effort to look at the positive in every situation.

Each year brings new milestones that mean the world to **our** family, even if they don't seem very significant to others. The kids are constantly surprising us and year by year we successfully accomplish things that at one stage were downright impossible!

Camping Trip with Friends

A group of our friends invited us to go camping for a weekend and we decided to accept without any hesitation. It really could not have gone better. The kids were calm, comfortable in new surroundings, had great fun and there were no dramas during the whole weekend.

Despite the unbelievable excitement that we could finally enjoy a weekend away with other families there were still moments where I was punishing myself and making comparisons with the other children and families. Even though our kids have progressed dramatically, it was obvious that they were not like all of the other kids. Most of the weekend, they were happy playing on their own, engrossed in their own world. I was constantly reassuring myself that it's okay, they are happy and have come so far but it's hard to leave those comparisons aside.

While other parents were talking about how their kids argued during the car ride and constantly asking, "How long till we get there?" and generally not giving them a moment's peace. I couldn't help thinking, "We don't have that problem, our kids don't even really speak," as a negative comparison.

During the weekend as we heard various children dobbing to their parents about the behaviour of other kids. I caught myself thinking sadly, "That's another thing we haven't experienced as parents." It was just so hard to keep reminding myself that these 'normal' struggles were things I didn't really have to worry about. Of course, that is easier said than done!

Thomas absolutely loved climbing in a big tree and being around the camp fire. Madi enjoyed riding her bike, swimming at the beach and surfing. Both kids loved the outdoors and the sense of adventure and space. My husband and I loved the sense of normalcy and hanging out with friends. Overall it was a major success.

Chapter Seventeen

Nurturing Understanding

"Have you ever wondered what it
can feel like to have autism?
Imagine being alone, in a large
and noisy foreign city — you can
understand a few words, but you
don't speak the language fluently.
The slightest noise can be distressing
and you desperately need to ask someone
for help... But you can't! This is what
it can feel like in a normal environment
for someone on the spectrum."

~ FB/Awareness for Autism

An Unexpected Gift

I have always had a million thoughts
Running through my head
So, one day I decided to write them down
And put them on paper instead

I have experienced so much in life
And so, I now have a lot to say
It's been a major form of therapy
To write things down this way

Now if I can help others
Or inspire someone else too
All the pains meant something more
Than what we have had to live through

I am up and I am down
But I still feel truly blessed
That I have experienced true love on every level
And to that I can attest

~ MONIQUE CAIN

Madi was in her second year of four-year-old kinder when a small boy said to me one morning "Madi is dumb and doesn't know anything." It was like a dagger through my heart and I honestly didn't know what to say, especially to a five-year old. I just said "Madi is not dumb, she just doesn't talk very much." There was so much more I could have said but I was shocked, defensive, heartbroken and guilt-ridden all at the same time.

Soon after that I began writing about life, emotions, and exploring what I thought was going on inside Madi's head. A poem turned into a story and I thought that if I put photos of Madi at kinder together with this story, both the kids and teachers might understand her better. And so, "Madi at Kinder" was born.

I went to Kmart-online, put my pictures and story together and showed it to Madi's teacher, who loved it and read it aloud to the class. She said there was nothing like that out there for kids and it helped them to understand Madi better. She kept the book in the classroom for the kids to look at if ever they had any questions.

The Next Madi Book...

Against her kinder teacher's well-meant advice (and with much fear and trepidation on our part), Madi went off to mainstream school the following year. After her experience at kinder I showed her teacher the book I had written and shared how helpful it had been. Her teacher loved the idea and showed "Madi at Kinder" to the principal who asked every teacher in the school to read the book aloud to their class. Now the whole school knew about Madi, and they were also more educated about autism in general and would hopefully be more kind, understanding and friendly to any kid that might seem a bit different. Some of the kids went home and talked about the book with their parents, and parents even asked to read it.

After such a positive response from the initial book I continued writing more books about Madi to help her classmates and their parents as well as her teachers understand the things she couldn't communicate. They were helpful and quite unique and eventually The Everyday Autism Series consisting of "Madi", "Madi at Kinder", "Madi at School", "Madi Goes Shopping", and, most recently, "I Am Thomas" were written and professionally illustrated and published to spread the message more widely.

The books are intended to be entertaining and informative, simple enough for children to read and understand, but helpful for adults too. These are the books we would have loved to be able to read ourselves and share with family and friends when our children were diagnosed with ASD. They would have saved us a lot of heartache.

In addition to the books, I use my website (https:// theeverydayautismseries.com.au/), Facebook page (https://www. facebook.com/theeverydayautismseries/), Instagram (https://www. instagram.com/theeverydayautismseries/) and other social media to blog about our kids and pass on relevant information to help raise awareness, provide understanding, and give hope to other families living with Autism.

From Little Things, Big Things Grow

Who would ever have thought that my children's autism would help me find my mission?

I never really knew exactly what I wanted to do professionally. I was a dance teacher, and have dabbled in a few different things, but mainly worked in our family's accounting business because it was an easy choice rather than my passion. Over the years I had written little bits and pieces, but it was more of a hobby than anything else. From time to time I casually thought that I could write a book or do something that would help people and change their lives for the better, but I never imagined it would work out this way.

I feel like I have turned what had been such a negative in our lives into a major positive not just for myself, but for Madi and other kids with autism. I am really proud of what I have been able to achieve so far and look forward to doing even more. I have given my children (and other children like them) a voice, so that those around them have greater understanding and awareness. It comforts me to know that by sharing Madi's and Thomas's stories I can help other children and families and make their experience a little bit easier. It is my hope that the picture books will help prevent bullying to some extent and help other adults to be less judgemental, kinder, more open, and friendlier. This is how I can make a difference in this world.

This book about our journey grew from the Madi books. As I have spoken at seminars and talked with other parents I realised that my own journey resonates with them. We all try so hard to hold everything together and summon up the courage to face another day, and now that I am finally back in a good mental state where I can make the things I want happen, I am ready to share what I can. After a period where my only respite came from drinking, my brain is finally clear and active again, so all the words I've scribbled on bits of paper are falling into place ready (I hope) to be the sustaining message of hope people need to hear.

I have currently sold books to every state in Australia and worldwide to New Zealand and the UK. I had the pleasure of being interviewed on channel 7's the afternoon edition, was a guest speaker at the 2017 ABA Today conference, wrote an article for Peninsula Kids Magazine, podcast radio interviews, daycare center book readings, a book review and advertisement in Melbourne Child Magazine and just recently landed a regular blogging gig with Source Kids, an online and Australian wide Special Needs publication.

So far, my books are available for purchase on my website (https://theeverydayautismseries.com.au/), various local bookstores, different speech therapists, local libraries, My Diffability Australia, which is an online special needs resource website, Early Childhood Australia, Everyday Kids, and Amazon Kindle to name a few.

I have already donated hundreds of books to various charities and organisations to help them raise money and am constantly fundraising and advocating for different Autism causes and foundations, having raised over $50,000 dollars to date.

My major goal is to have my books present in all kinders, schools, day care centers and homes worldwide because I believe that every child deserves a chance to be understood and appreciated for who they are.

Chapter Eighteen

The Many Ways of Showing Affection

"If you enter this world knowing that
you are loved and leave this world
knowing the same, then everything
in between can be dealt with."

~ MICHAEL JACKSON

I know a lot of children on the spectrum aren't comfortable with physical demonstrations of affection... what is less commonly stated is that a lot of children who are **not** on the spectrum don't like lots of hugs and kisses either. There are definitely times we need to give our kids their own space. We have learned to gauge when those times are necessary. We have also learned to accept and enjoy their occasionally rough and exuberant physical displays of affection and to appreciate how precious they are, especially after several years when they avoided such contact.

There are also lots of ways of showing affection that don't invade their space. We've tried to be very creative and intentional about communicating love to our children and I think as a result, they are super-affectionate in return. I truly believe that endless and unconditional love has had a really positive impact in so many ways. They know that we love them for who they are, no matter what and that we are trying our best to understand and respond to them even when we are helping them learn new things and behaviours.

We've tried to find different ways of doing things that to us represent 'good parenting' like reading aloud at bedtime. So, when it was nearly impossible to read to both kids at night before bed, we would sing to them instead. We tried singing and dance actions for just about everything in fact, whether it was on the trampoline, on the swing, in the house, or driving in the car, to encourage interaction, learning, and speech. Whether it was a known song or made up rhyme, they seemed to enjoy it and respond positively.

Early on it seemed as though we were always trying to teach, train, and rebuke our children to make them fit in with socially acceptable behaviours and it was hard to find rewards that were meaningful to them. We've come a long way on this, but we are still experimenting and looking for more ways of showing our unconditional love.

We wasted a lot of time trying to get them to make eye-contact with strangers, not realising how difficult that is for people with autism. People used to say that the eyes were the windows to the soul and it's natural to want to hide the depths of our soul from random strangers. Maybe we also need to ask if it's natural to want to peer into other people's souls, especially if we are super-sensitive to their emotions. Now, we know the value of the gift our children are giving when they look straight into our eyes and let us look into theirs.

I have now come to the conclusion that the most important thing for my children is their happiness. I want them to know they are loved no matter how they behave or what they can and cannot do... because we really do love them unconditionally. That's why it's so important for us to keep learning about autism, and to help others understand it too. Now that we are more educated about autism and how they must be feeling, we can judge their true wants and needs much better. To look into their eyes and see them beaming back at me, to see their genuine smile and giggles is all the reassurance I need. I no longer need them to be able to verbally express how they are feeling although it would be nice, I can tell just by observing them.

Chapter Nineteen

What Makes a Good Parent?

"When your child is having a MELTDOWN
Don't talk
Don't try to reason
Don't get angry
Your child can't hear you
Just be silent and loving until
the storm passes."

~ SUE LARKY

I wish I had seen this quote or read something along these lines in the early days of our parenting... it's good advice even if your child doesn't have autism or hasn't been diagnosed. It would have saved us a lot of pain and tears. We did learn after a long time, the hard way. It's still a challenge to keep your cool while the storm is raging and remember that the storm will pass.

Both our kids, but particularly Madi, have gone through many phases of behaviour that have been really hard to deal with. With time, thankfully, the majority of them have passed and then the next one comes. The hardest part about it for me is the sense of judgement you receive from others. I always feel as though I need to explain what is going on so that I won't see that look of disapproval in the eyes of strangers.

When Madi was younger she had a funny obsession with pillows. She had to take one everywhere and it had to be covered with one of grandma's daggy floral pillow cases. At that time, she also wanted to wear her daddy's t-shirts all the time. So, at age three, when she started regular therapy, that is how she would arrive. Dressed in daddy's t-shirt with pillow in hand!

Madi also had issues if her clothing got wet. She couldn't handle the sensation and would have to instantly strip. We soon learned that we needed to have a spare dress with us everywhere we went in case she needed to change. One day I thought, we're just going to quickly run into the bank, so I won't need to take a change. Stupidly I also let her take a bottle of water... It did cross my mind that this might be a big mistake, but I foolishly ignored that fleeting thought. Standing in line, Madi took a sip of water, spilled it, and needed to take her dress off! I did all I could to get her to leave it on, even physically pulling it down, and all the time she was getting increasingly upset. People were staring, judging, and I am feeling like a total failure. I'm such a bad parent, so incompetent that I can't even quickly run into the bank. We didn't even make it to the teller. I left the bank trying to shield Madi as she walked out naked to the car. What does a good parent do in this situation?

There was a long period of time where Madi refused to wear a seat belt. I would have to pull over repeatedly, reach over to fasten her seatbelt while driving, or yell at her to leave it fastened. It was frightening, but I didn't know what to do since most of our trips involved taking her to essential appointments. We received many dirty looks when people noticed as they drove past. I thought about creating a car sticker to explain. Thankfully that stage passed too and now she puts on her seatbelt as well as her brother's as soon as we enter the car without being asked.

At another time Madi liked to stick her head out of the car window, just like a dog. Thank God for driver window lock, it was really scary sometimes! Then she discovered the sun roof. The wind flowing through her hair, the sun on her face... the look on her face was one of pure joy! I think it must have been a major sensory release as well as sheer fun. I would only allow her to do this when we were on our own very quiet street. One day, while Madi was enjoying her few moments of fresh air and freedom a man drove past us in his golf buggy. He turned his buggy around and followed us to our house then parked beside me in my driveway. I took the kids inside and went back out to see what he wanted.

As I approached him, he started to question my parenting and challenged me for allowing my child to do such a thing. I felt defensive but tried to keep my cool while I was being abused in my own driveway. In hindsight, I could have handled the situation better, but I was already struggling mentally and emotionally and here was a complete stranger who had followed me to my own house to attack my parenting skills. I tried to respond calmly with, "You don't know me, and you don't know what my life is like, so you really aren't in a position to comment," but he just kept on criticising. Eventually an overwhelming rush of adrenaline came over me and I literally screamed at him, "My daughter is autistic!"

Quick as a flash, he jumped back in his golf buggy and drove away. I was shocked, shaking, nearly hysterical, and completely bewildered at what had just transpired and I still had to take care of my babies. Luckily my husband was able to come home early from work to comfort me.

There were other issues along the way. Ripping paper has been an issue for both kids. Madi would rip all the pages of her reading/picture books. I would get upset and annoyed by the waste... and, of course, there was the fear that they would damage someone else's property. She and Thomas both used to occasionally chew random bits of paper. Thomas has always had an obsession with ripping paper into strips. Every day my floors were completely covered with strips of torn paper, but that has now progressed to flocks of paper birds and dragons, or fleets of pirate ships.

Probably the most concerning phase, was when Madi was toilet training and she would do her number two's on the carpet. OMG, it was disgusting! It went on for a lengthy amount of time and no matter what we tried to do to prevent it from happening nothing worked. In the end we bought our own heavy-duty steam cleaner. Then, one day it just stopped, she began going to the toilet without further problems.

All of these things were seriously stressful as we were experiencing them. Now that we are in a better place it is easier to be more relaxed when these new phases arise. I try to remind myself that this too will pass.

As a special needs parent, you are constantly questioning your parenting skills. It's really important not to try and think too far ahead. You need to take it day by day and never give up. There will be good days and bad ones but the future is unknown. With all the help, support, technology, awareness and progress, you just never know what may be possible.

National Disability Insurance Scheme (NDIS)

This is going to transform the lives of many families with special needs kids! So many more families will now be able to get much-needed help and support in Australia as this program is rolled out. We were fortunate to be able to pay for most of the early interventions we needed, but many families are not in a position to do so. I wish it had been available sooner, but it will be a continued life-long support for our kids, and I hope that all families will investigate and make the most of this amazingly generous initiative from our government.

It is seriously depressing to think that you need a whole team of professionals to help you look after your own children. It's humiliating to think that what ought to be a perfectly natural process of children learning, communicating, and interacting with their parents and the world takes so many outside interventions. We have been so lucky to have had such a supportive network of family and friends, but they knew as much about Autism as we did, which was nothing. We could talk to them, cry on their shoulder from time to time, but we needed more than that.

There are so many aspects to diagnosis and treatment, so much paperwork and so many different appointments that the whole process is intensely draining and exhausting both emotionally and physically without wondering what you can afford.

A Strong Marriage is an Important Foundation

They say parenting isn't for cowards. Parenting a child with autism certainly isn't. Thankfully my husband and I had an extremely strong bond before we had kids and embarked on this autism journey. Even so, it hasn't been easy, and our relationship has been seriously tested at times.

For several years, it seemed as though we were never both in a good place at the same time, but we have been able to support each other through the good times and the bad, so I guess you could also say that we were never both in a really bad place at the same time, either. He is the only person who really knows how I feel, as we have ridden all the waves together. I certainly feel now, more than ever, that because of all we have endured together, we are a force to be reckoned with and can conquer whatever lies ahead. I'm so grateful for that. A lot of families don't make it through situations like this, but I feel our love is deeper and stronger than ever. Together we make an unbreakable team.

Embracing Our Children's Differences

Yes, every child is different. Every parent is also different from other parents and we certainly haven't done everything right or all that was possible, but we have done the very best that we could at the time. I found it really helped me once I learned to accept that I wasn't the perfect parent with the perfect kids that were bathed, fed and in bed by seven every night. In fact, I realised that there was no such thing as perfection in parenting. There is only the loving of the children we have.

I struggled for so long to avoid criticism and judgement when my children were in public and to follow our society's many unwritten rules and expectations that I felt we needed to abide by. Eventually I started to question these. Why do we need to do that? Who says that kids should be saying so many words by a certain age? Who decrees what foods children should eat? What time they should go to bed? That they have to have friends or play with other kids?

So, Madi and Thomas don't like wearing shoes or extra layers of clothing. Does it matter? If they feel cold then they put more clothes on, and if they are comfortable then why should they wear more layers? How would you feel if people were constantly forcing you to do things that you didn't really like, that made you feel uncomfortable, or that you simply didn't want to do? And, is there any reason why it's OK to force you into those things just because you can't verbally communicate your reasons.

"Why fit in when you can stand out?"
~ Dr. Seuss

I have come to believe that good parenting demands that we encourage our children to be themselves, to explore their unique abilities and differences, and that we **stop** requiring them to fit in with others. Recognising that gives me the reassurance I always wanted, that I am doing the right thing as their mother. It's not their achievements or conformity that qualifies me as a good parent: whether they play sport, win academic prizes, or wear beautiful dresses and headbands (not that these are bad things); the only really important qualification is that they know in their hearts that I will never give up on them, I will always be there for them, that they are truly loved, and that I will do anything and everything in my power to help them become their true selves.

Chapter Twenty

Self-Nurture

"At times our own light goes out and
is rekindled by a spark from another
person. Each of us has cause to think
with deep gratitude of those who
have lighted the flame within us."

~ ALBERT SCHWEITZER

The Depths of Misery and the Spectre of Despair

I used to think that the best thing I could do was soldier on. Do
what needed to be done. Avoid making demands on others. Give
my kids and husband everything they needed. Pretend that alcohol,
sleep, and time were all I needed to cope with the hand life was
dealing me. I was wrong.

After a while, the demands of life took their toll. I was broken
inside. Outwardly, I was still functioning, working, looking after
the kids, running the household, doing what needed to be done,
but inside I was writhing in silent agony. I was drinking too much,
too often. Sometimes, I would drink to excess and either end up

curled up in a ball in the shower or cry myself to sleep. Sometimes I did both. Many nights I would hear my husband sobbing in the other room. I didn't go to him... I couldn't bear his misery as well as my own. I couldn't talk to anyone about my kids without breaking down in tears, not even their father... my husband.

At times, I would obsessively clean the house. I probably should have been spending every waking moment teaching or helping my children, but I felt a compulsive need to clean. I think maybe unconsciously, it was the one thing I could control... a coping mechanism of sorts.

Most of the time I hid my state very well. Few people realised how broken I really was because I knew I just had to get up and keep going everyday regardless, for my kids.

Seeking Professional Help for Yourself

We were so busy seeking professional help for our kids, appreciating the skill and knowledge they had to offer, but we ignored our own needs... possibly another form of denial.

One night, as I lay in the shower curled up in a ball of misery sobbing, after another evening drinking too much I realised that I was heading down a road to a very dark place. That was the moment I decided I didn't want to be unhappy anymore and was ready to see a counsellor for my own sake and for the sake of my kids.

The whole process was very confronting and emotional, but it was a major turning point and the best thing I could have done. I cried through all of my early counselling sessions but talking to someone outside the situation really helped me and enabled me to release a lot of weight off my chest. I cleansed my soul... and there was a lot of cleansing to do. I have been so lucky to have been blessed with truly amazing friends, that I could talk to and confide in, but during these years I stopped talking to them because I felt bad about always complaining and being negative.

Confiding in a professional was a lot easier than I expected and I was able to be totally and brutally honest with myself about how I truly felt. I could say anything to her and not feel judged. It didn't feel as though I was talking like a broken record. She knew exactly what to suggest and how to draw the appropriate responses out of me and she would respond back with comfort and reassurance. She assured me that it was OK and completely normal to feel like I was cheated. To feel angry, sad, defeated, and devastated. She said a lot of people experience this like a 'grieving process' and she was right. That is exactly what it has been like. Grieving for the life you thought you were going to enjoy as a mother and a family... the life you thought your children would enjoy.

She asked me if I liked writing. Over the years I had written bits and pieces, mostly journal content, and a few good stories at school. She encouraged me to write and gave me homework to work on in between sessions. It was the absolute perfect thing for me. Writing became my primary form of therapy. My mental state and whole outlook really improved. Maybe it wasn't obvious on the outside, but I knew things had changed.

Work on Your Happiness

Autistic children are especially sensitive to atmosphere. It's probably one of the reasons why they struggle in public places and crowds. I believe it's even more important for parents of autistic children to prioritise their own happiness for others.

Your children pick up negative emotions and atmosphere even when you wear a cheerful facade. I think there is a direct correlation between my own self-care and internal healing and the dramatic improvements we have seen in our children.

Never Did I Imagine

Never did I imagine
That things would be this hard
To smile and get on with it
Putting on a fake facade

It's meant to be a great time
The best time of your life
To have a family
After becoming husband and wife

Experience all the joys
Of watching children grow
Be excited about the future
And responsible for what they know

Except it didn't happen
The way we thought it should
Thrown curve balls and devastating news
Not the excitement we thought we would

Not wanting to get out of bed
To face the world, the truth
That all our hopes and dreams were shattered
By our children's complex youth.
~ MONIQUE CAIN

Chapter Twenty-One

What's Next?

"What would happen if the autism gene was eliminated from the gene pool? You would have a bunch of people standing around in a cave, chatting and socialising and not getting anything done."

~ DR TEMPLE GRANDIN

I love this quotation. It reminds me of how much difference people with autism have made in this world… and that's just the ones we know about. It reminds me that autism is not a disease. It's a difference… and this world surely needs people who will make a difference.

Every year for the past few years I have reflected on all of the things we have been able to achieve as a family, especially this year and how far the kids have come. Each year it feels quite surreal, but I honestly could not be happier. Each year there are new accomplishments that at one stage I thought would never be possible. We have now reached so many major milestones, that we no longer hesitate when contemplating future possibilities. I have an overwhelming sense of pride and, after so many negative experiences, I feel we are finally getting to enjoy some of the true joys of family life and parenting.

When I think back to the day of our initial diagnosis when the doctor said with devastating honesty that he couldn't predict whether Madi would ever speak, be continent, tolerate groups, feed herself, or achieve any other milestones I'm in awe of what we've accomplished, and I do believe that anything is possible.

Let's look at the list so far:

- Toilet training
- Obedience and ability to sit still
- Using cutlery and feeding themselves
- Participating in school activities and concerts
- Getting invited to birthday parties (and attending them)
- Learning to stand in line
- Attending mainstream kinder and school
- Starting to read
- Camping
- Travelling overseas
- Visiting the zoo, theme parks, and other attractions
- Learning to ride a bike
- Learning to respond verbally with appropriate language
- Visiting friends and talking to strangers
- Trying new foods
- Wearing dress-ups
- Surfing

I could keep going. It hasn't been an easy road to get to this point, which I guess makes it all the sweeter. It has taken a lot of blood, sweat and tears to get here, but everything is slowly coming together. We still face many challenges, but life is so much easier than it used to be, and we can actually enjoy ourselves and have fun.

Parenting and having children hasn't been anything like the picture I had in my mind, but we have come such a long way and we are sharing some joyous moments together. I feel like we have turned what was such a negative in our lives into a positive. I have found a new purpose. I take great comfort in the fact that our children are happy and loved and we can now help other people with their journeys too.

As hard as things have been (and will continue to be), my children continue to inspire me to be the best mother I can be. And, with all their difficulties, they continue to surprise us all the time by trying to be the best that they can be too. I hope I can also inspire other parents with my story.

Never give up, no matter how hard things may be and do everything possible to make the best out of your given situation. You never know what will happen next... and it may be more wonderful than you can ever imagine.

PART TWO

Tips for Dealing with Daily Life

"Negative words carry negative vibration. Positive words carry positive vibration. What do you want your child to reflect back to you, the label of disordered or the label of gifted in a new way?"

~ SUZY MILLER, AWESOMISM

Chapter Twenty-Three

Bedtime and Sleep Routines

"Behaviour is communication. Change the
environment and behaviours will change"

~ LANA DAVID

Bedtime and sleep routines are frequently difficult for parents of kids with autism. It's not just that our kids need sleep, it's that we need sleep ourselves and the more sleep-deprived we become the more we struggle to cope with the challenges of daily life.

I don't know that we have answers, I do know that as a parent who struggled with bedtime every night, I loved hearing other people's solutions and struggles.

I honestly don't know how we survived or kept functioning properly with the years of interrupted sleep, but we did. Some nights we barely slept at all, other nights we stayed up until ten, eleven, or even twelve o'clock. We went through stages when the kids would refuse to have a bath or shower, and others when they wanted four per day. Teeth-brushing time could drive them to near hysteria. They didn't have the attention span or the patience to sit and listen to a book being read to them, nor could they go to sleep on their own or stay asleep all night in their own bed.

We ended up so tired, emotional, and frustrated, that we often gave in because it all got too hard and then we felt like an absolute failure as a parent. I mean, other parents manage, don't they?

We tried lots of different options or tactics, but nothing was working for us. Melatonin, a perfect solution for some parents, was torture to get down and did not have a lasting effect. Finally, we accepted the fact that we were not going to get our kids fed, bathed, read to, and in bed for the night by 7:00pm and put double beds in all of our bedrooms, so we could at least get some sort of sleep. We had to become a lot more relaxed with our expectations and do what we could to survive.

I think it helps that they are now a bit older, more understanding and aware, and so much more comfortable in the world and in themselves that they are just more prepared to comply because over the past year we have seen a lot of improvement. We have worked on several of the pre-bed elements separately like having a toothbrush tolerance program and step-by-step progress to reading books.

This year developing a bedtime routine was a major goal and we approached it slowly. Both kids are now happy to have either a bath or shower. Then, at approximately 8.30pm, it's 'bedtime', which they verbally repeat. So, we all go upstairs, and they brush their teeth (using electric toothbrushes which are quite fun) and then rinsing properly, too. The electric toothbrushes were quite a hit when we introduced them. Toilet is next, before they each hop into their own beds and read their school readers to us. We are still working on going to sleep at a reasonable hour, but this is a monumental start! After reading with Madi, I have been applying some essential oils, then I scratch or stroke her for a short time until she goes off to sleep. Thomas is now happy to lie in his bed by himself and usually drifts off to sleep while watching a movie. Most nights he sleeps through the night, but Madi still wakes up frequently during the night and comes into our room. We are being consistent, taking her back to her own bed and settling her down again.

I know it is far from perfect, but it is so much better than it was! A few times Madi has actually told us that she is tired and wants to go to bed! The simple joys of an autism parent... LOL!

We do try to stick to a basic routine because ASD kids tend to thrive in a structured environment. The kids love to go straight home after school and If I attempt to go to the shops, it will more often than not result in a melt own or erratic behavior. It helps us all to stay calm when we keep a similar schedule even if we occasionally slip in some flexibility.

Chapter Twenty-Four

Food

"It is never too late to expand the mind of a person on the autism spectrum."

~ DR. TEMPLE GRANDIN

A lot of ASD kids have sensory issues relating to different foods. Their response may be related to the look, smell, or taste of different elements and they may experience some degree of anxiety as a result of any of those issues.

Our kids like to eat the same foods over and over again and they do not tolerate any changes, no matter how slight, in the look or taste of their preferred food. Thomas loved a particular Woolworths brand of muesli bar. When they changed the packaging and made a slight change to the top of the bar, he stopped eating them.

Some of the helpful tips I've gathered to help your child experiment and avoid massive food issues include: -

- Imitate eating and encourage a good social and interactive eating experience at every meal.
- Involve your child in all aspects of the meal: preparation, cooking, and eating.

- Don't discipline your child at meal time to avoid a negative experience.
- Establish a regular eating routine with meals regularly served at the same place, same time, same manner.
- Make a habit of regular family meals.
- Use shared plates to encourage your children to choose their own food.
- Don't have high expectations. Ask them to eat just three foods: one protein, one carbohydrate, and one fruit or vegetable.
- Let them spit food out and praise them for trying it, but then encourage them to put it in the bin and try another piece.
- Talk about the idea that 'food is fuel'.
- Be patient and persevere.

Chapter Twenty-Five

Birthdays

"Within every living child exists the most
precious bud of self-identity. To search this
out and foster it with loving care; that is
the essence of educating an autistic child"

~ Dr. Kiyo Kitahara

For most children and families, birthdays are a very special occasion. They can be some of the most memorable days of our lives. The anticipation, seeing your children's expectant faces and the excited reaction to presents and celebrations with family and friends is all part of the thrill.

But that certainly has not been the case for our little family so far. I have found these days along with the weeks leading up to them, to be some of the most mentally challenging. We have no build up towards the date of the birth, no counting how many sleeps or anticipation of how old they will be. There are no requests for specific toys they want, no discussion of who will come to their party, or what their preferred cake or party theme might be.

Looking back, one of the earliest pre-diagnosis memories of my daughter Madi was at her second birthday party. We held it at a local park, and I noticed that she was not at all interested in playing with the other kids, she was happiest playing by herself. She was not interested in opening any of her birthday presents, nor did she care what was inside the parcel when she finally did open them. All our parties since have had a similar outcome. There has been limited interaction with other kids, minimal interest in playing party games, no indication of wanting presents, and they have sometimes hidden in another room to avoid the people and the noise.

As a parent I feel overcome with guilt if I don't at least attempt to make an effort to acknowledge the occasion yet in the end, they have turned out to be more hassle and heartache than they are worth.

Both kids have been invited to other kid's parties. It is lovely to be included, but our first attempts didn't end well. After a few awkward incidents we developed a few rules. We would arrive a little bit late and our goal would be to stay for just one hour. That way we had at least made the effort.

In 2017, instead of a birthday party for Thomas, we decided to take him to the zoo. We thought it was a better option considering his profound love of animals and dislike of people and parties. We pre-booked our tickets online, so we didn't have to queue. We arrived early, as the gates were opening, and avoided the massive crowds. We had our survival backpacks on hand with all essentials in case of any emergencies.

It was the best family/kids' day out we have ever had! The look on Thomas's face was priceless, he was so happy and excited! He was allowed to pick some soft toys from the gift shop there for presents. He absolutely loved the animal zoo map, since he's a massive fan of Dora the Explorer.

All day we said, "Happy birthday, Thomas." "Thomas, it's your birthday," and "Thomas, you are six today," to help reinforce the fact of his birthday and the reason for the celebration. He was happy to have the "Happy Birthday" song, to blow out candles, and was even interested in opening his presents. It was the best birthday ever, a day we will always cherish and never forget!

Chapter Twenty-Six

Christmas

"Even for parents of children who
are not on the spectrum, there is
no such thing as a normal child."

~ VIOLET STEVENS

Over the past few years Christmas has been a difficult day in our house. The kids have shown little to no interest in presents or the whole occasion. We haven't felt as though we have been able to experience the true joy that children usually bring to the festive season. During the past year our kids have begun to show a lot more interest in various occasions and events. Once again, we tried to prepare them as much as possible, by watching kids' Christmas movies, reading related books, and regularly talking about Santa's visit. We decided to split the days with our families because it has been too much of everything all on one day. Finally, in 2017, we were pleasantly surprised and absolutely overwhelmed with emotion with what occurred.

After some initial encouragement, both kids were excited to open their presents. They played with them, showed genuine happiness and joy, and were affectionately thankful when prompted. Madi had another food first, when she sampled her first taste of pavlova. She has such a sweet tooth! The simple presents were the ones they liked most, including a bubble machine that provided hours of fun and entertainment.

Our absolute highlight was when Madi sang for us all! This is a child that was completely non-verbal just a few years ago, doesn't willingly speak and can't hold a normal conversation, but now loves to sing songs from kids' movies. Her Nan decided to buy her a karaoke machine to see how that would go. We bought the music CD soundtracks from a few of her recent favourite movies, *Moana* and *Trolls* and the songs that she has been singing to go with it. She absolutely loved it! Even more, she really got into the whole performance, holding the notes and being animated with her hands, face, and body movements.

We were hopeful and even quietly confident that the karaoke machine might go down well but this went beyond our wildest dreams. The whole family were in tears with happiness. We just could not believe it, coming from where we have been... The best Christmas present we could ever dream for us all! A moment in time we will always treasure and never forget. We have learnt that finding what the kids are passionate about and running with it, as farfetched as it may seem, is having major rewards. It just goes to show once again, never give up hope because you just never know what's around the corner... and, when you see they have an interest, encourage them and let them pursue it.

Chapter Twenty-Seven

Interaction and Inclusion

"Autism is really more of a difference to be worked with rather than a monolithic enemy that needs to be slain or destroyed."

~ STEPHEN SHORE, PHD

The developmental value of including children with ASD in mainstream activities as far as possible is widely known. The benefit for 'ordinary' kids is an unparalleled opportunity to learn how to relate to people with different strengths, gifts, and behaviours... something every human being needs to learn.

From a very young age it was clear that my daughter Madi was different. She was unable to connect or engage with others and seemed trapped in her own world. Things like mainstream kinder were extremely difficult for her. It was easy for other kids to build relationships, participate in concerts or excursions, and learn to follow rules, but Madi really struggled to co-exist and became quite isolated at times as a result.

The main point I want to get across in my children's books is the importance of being kind, friendly, and inclusive of kids with ASD as well as any child that may act a bit differently. No matter what it looks like from the outside you would be surprised at how much they actually do recognise and absorb. Some of their unusual behaviour is the result of not feeling comfortable and needing time to adjust, but they may not be able to verbalize that fact. I wanted to provide logical reasons for what is often judged as odd behaviour in simple language. I wanted people to know that all children can learn, but not everyone learns new skills at the same speed. I also wanted people to realise that certain things (noise, change, light, smells, etc.) may strongly disturb some people so that they behave in ways that seem unusual, and that there are many different ways of communicating.

My original intention was simply to communicate this to Madi's friends and teachers, but when I received such an encouraging response, I wanted to give other parents and families access to this resource in the hope that it will smooth their path to inclusion. Kids learn quickly and the earlier they understand that ASD kids are people too and that they gain knowledge and confidence through inclusion the more natural it will be for them. All the teachers I have spoken to are also keen to embrace and explore different ways of learning and forms of inclusion.

There is certainly a lot more awareness and influence on inclusion in mainstream school these days. Hopefully with the assistance of *"The Everyday Autism Series,"* that will continue to increase. Kids are more accepting, and teachers are more understanding and accommodating. Another special needs parent and Occupational Therapist said to me that this is the real world, where all kids have to integrate, special needs and

all, so it is exposing everyone to a more realistic situation…
and she is right!

Madi's grade teacher this year said to me that most of the
kids in her class are at different levels academically, so she caters
for each individual anyway. There are so many new and improved
learning and teaching techniques being used across the board to
help all children learn in different ways, which I love!

With aides assisting and more sensory awareness and relief for
every child, they all have more opportunities to learn… if you find
the right school for your child. We could not be any luckier, since
our perfect school is literally down the road from where we live!
I know some people who travel for hours each day, move towns,
or even move states and countries to find the best school for their
child and they are truly worth it!

We are still really unsure if the kids will continue in mainstream
school down the track but we will see how everything goes. The
school has been fantastic about putting things in place to
help our children cope and be as free from distraction and as
comfortable as possible. They've been great about allowing the
kids to have fidget toys and use relaxation techniques or breaks
in a safe, quiet room.

Some Simple Things You Can Do (and Teach Others to Do)

- Keep saying, "Hi," everyday even if you don't get a response back;
- Sit next to them when you eat your snack or play a game.
  Persevere even if they don't seem to respond;

- Give them a high five or ask if you can join in their play. One day they might just respond or join in with you;
- Play alongside them so that they get used to you and become more comfortable;
- Be careful not to invade their personal space, especially if you have not been invited;
- Be patient (as much as you can be at the time). Keep asking and approaching them, whether it's in five minutes, next week, next month, or next year;
- Speak very slowly, clearly, simply, and not too loudly. In a classroom or playground there are a lot of other noises to contend with which makes it hard for children on the spectrum to concentrate or focus on one particular thing.

Perseverance and repetition are very important. Thomas did not want to ride his bike at all for years. However, at different stages we kept inviting him to try and now he loves it.

In a classroom setting, ASD kids often interact better in smaller groups because too many people can be overwhelming. Ideally, you want to provide a quiet place where a child can escape and take a break from all the chaos, if they need one.

We set some personal goals or rules for ourselves to follow when we were out and about or at public occasions like family days or birthday parties. We would aim to stay for an hour. If there was some incident before then and we had to leave early we did so, but at least we had made the effort to go. Initially if we reached that one-hour goal, we would leave immediately to ensure that the kids had a positive experience. Eventually, we would stay longer if the kids were comfortable, but we are always ready to abort at any sign of difficulty.

Madi's Experience

At the end of the day the decision to put your ASD child in mainstream school is one of the many decisions every parent has to make for themselves. We were terrified of making the wrong choice.

When the time came for us to make our decision about where Madi would go to school we were faced with conflicting opinions. Her kinder teacher was strongly encouraging us to send her to a special school, not believing that she would be able to cope in a mainstream school environment. Madi's ABA therapists were of the total opposite opinion, thinking that she would in fact benefit from learning in a mainstream setting. We ended up taking the approach that we would try mainstream first and if that didn't work, we could always change schools.

The first year of prep was quite challenging and Madi faced a lot of the same issues as she had at kinder, including becoming comfortable with her surroundings. However, she was definitely making progress, so we started her in Grade 1. That year she began to form some friendships, was more engaged in class, and more relaxed. In her third year at mainstream school, she blew us away with her progress! The transition into Grade 2 was relatively seamless and she chose to actively participate on a daily basis, and engage more with her classmates, teachers, aides and other students. She was learning on a similar level and assigned the same class work to complete. She had kids inviting her to birthday parties and asking her to have play dates with them as well as receiving awards and participating in all school activities. The school principal even said to me "This is the place Madi should be."

If she hadn't been given this opportunity of inclusion, we're not sure where she would be today. We really appreciate the additional challenge including Madi has posed for her teachers and will always be grateful for the way they have included her and treated her as a valued member of her class and the school. She is absolutely thriving because of it.

Every kid needs to be given a chance to shine. ASD kids simply need more time and patience to feel more comfortable and confident to explore life in our world.

Chapter Twenty-Eight

Sickness with Limited Speech

Each mother has different challenges,
Different skills and abilities,
And certainly, different children...
What matters is that a mother
loves her children deeply...

~ Elder M Russel Ballard

I t was back to school time on Monday morning after two weeks of school holidays. My son was visibly unhappy about it and quite clearly did not want to go to school. I just thought it was back to school blues because he loves to be at home doing his own thing and will often say, "No school," with occasional real tears. This time, that was not the case. I received a text and photo from his aide at 10am to let me know he was unwell.

This is definitely one of the hardest parts of this whole autism journey, the fact that our kids can't properly verbalise how they feel. Unless they are clearly looking as though they are practically on death's door, we are pretty much oblivious to their health conditions because they can't express how they are feeling. This makes Monday's incident really hard to judge.

It also makes me feel like a bad parent. Surely, I should have known that he wasn't well even if he couldn't say, "Mum, I feel sick." But I didn't.

Another major issue in dealing with our sick kids is that they will **not** take any sort of oral medication to help them get better. It has always been an absolute nightmare attempting to give them simple things like liquid Panadol. We literally have to hold them down and force it down their throats while they are gagging, screaming, crying, dry retching, and sometimes vomiting it back up. It's another one of those 'terrible parent' moments! Because of the need to physically restrain them and force the medicine down their throats we seriously evaluate the potential benefits of any medication.

Normally, we just ride it out and trust that, at the very least, they are building up a really good immune system. All things considered, they cope really well when they are sick. They usually just lie in bed and sleep on and off. Thankfully, they are pretty healthy kids and don't seem to get sick that often. When they do, it's like dealing with a baby. You know something is wrong but it's up to you to work out what the problem is and how serious it is.

This is one of those areas where you just have to refrain from judging yourself, accept that you are doing your best, and keep moving forward.

Chapter Twenty-Nine

TV & Screens

"I see people with Asperger's syndrome as
a bright thread in the rich tapestry of life."
~ TONY ATTWOOD

I know a lot of parents don't agree with their kids watching much TV or having screen time, but I think it helped our children learn to speak properly. They would repeat words and lines from their favourite movies and act them out as if they were playing the role in the movie. At one stage when Madi was not speaking at all and did not read or respond with words or phrases of her own, she could recite whole movies word for word.

It's like learning a foreign language. One of the most effective ways of learning to speak fluently in your own words is to hear and repeat other people's phrases over and over again until finally you start to think and feel the natural patterns of the language. For many autistic children, learning to put together meaningful sentences in their native language takes as much time, effort, and repetition, as learning a new language takes for most adults. It's just the way their brains are wired.

As far as I'm concerned, if a movie or other electronic devices will patiently repeat the words or information my child needs to hear or see as often as they need to hear and see it, it's a tool. I understand the concerns about screen time and its effect on children's brains, but when your child's brain is already wired differently your perspective is quite different.

Madi has learned so much from using her iPad! There are so many educational and entertaining apps available that focus on learning and speech. It has been extremely helpful at school and enabled her to learn people's names and faces, recognise letters, write, count, and so many other things. We used an amazing app called "Pro Lo Quo" that helped her to speak and communicate. Both our kids seem to be very visual learners and TV and iPads are very entertaining and engaging for children.

It's another one of those areas where I think each family needs to use their own judgement and decide what works best for their child.

Chapter Thirty

Give Them Time!

"The biggest gift you can give to people with autism is time."

~ Prof. Rita Jordan

I truly believe that time **is** the biggest influence for ASD kids on so many different levels! They need more time than many others to feel more comfortable in this world, in their surroundings, and in their own skin. Some adults with autism have described the learning journey in terms of visiting an alien planet: how can you learn while you are still trying to breathe?

In an increasingly hurried and impatient society, time is a very precious resource and anyone who slows down the pace may be brushed aside. All children would probably benefit from being given more time, yet children with autism absolutely need more time to learn, to show their strengths, to discover what they are good at, and what they love to do.

When the kids were first diagnosed and we initially started speech therapy, the kids weren't ready for that. We needed to start with more basic steps like being able to follow instructions first.

Now, several years later we are revisiting speech therapy because that is an appropriate next step.

I understand the challenge for classroom teachers who have a whole classroom of students to educate. Madi is now in Grade 3, yet she is probably only reading at Prep level. It's taking her more time than her classmates, but when she was actually in Prep she was pretty much non-verbal and struggling to speak. We realised that we just have to work at things at our own pace and not worry about the 'normal' rate for their age.

As parents we need to take the time to really get to know our own children's likes, dislikes, and triggers. Often, it's small things that make all the difference like cutting the seeds out of watermelon, putting their socks on inside out, and cutting off the tags on their underwear. We need to take the time to learn the signs that suggest how and when we can push or ask for more. This is not just a one-off discovery like completing a questionnaire or test, it's an on-going journey: working out what to do, who to see, as well as regularly reassessing your situation. Other parents may think (and say) that you are spoiling your child by pandering to their whims, when you do these things for them. I have learned to ignore these comments and just do what is best for my child… to help them adjust to this alien world.

Now, especially with the introduction of the NDIS, we have been encouraged to set new goals to work towards on an annual basis with the help and assistance of more therapies and therapists. It is good to have specific things to focus on and work towards because it can feel really overwhelming at times.

When our kids were little, we would often try to read them stories, but they were just not interested at all. They were unable to sit for any length of time, unable to pay attention to a story, would try to rip the book's pages, and evidently had no comprehension of the process. It took time, but things changed! Now Thomas will come over to me with a book in his hand and will say, "Read book." They are both happy to sit and listen to a story, ask questions, and even read aloud themselves. Every time we read to them, or we hear their voice read to us it is so surreal, and each experience is a very treasured moment!

Adjusting to new people, places, and things are always challenging along with any other form of change. Remembering to allow extra time for adjustment and not to rush things is extremely important.

Managing Expectations

It has taken some time to adjust our expectations of what we imagined all our lives would be like down to every tiny little aspect and it is ever-evolving.

Just when you get your head around not being able to pursue, get involved, experience, or adapt to something your kids may surprise you by reaching a new level of progress. Suddenly, you start to think, "Well, maybe it is possible and then what else might be possible next?" But then you go into self-protect mode: you don't want to get your hopes up for your dreams and expectations to be shattered once again.

Most of our expectations are now concerned with our children and family's general happiness. They may seem pretty simple to others, but they represent major achievements for us.

Chapter Thirty-One

School Holidays

"Routine is very important for people with autism. This doesn't mean that you can't change things, but that you need to expect a period of adjustment."

~ MONIQUE CAIN

We've noticed that over the school holidays Madi tends to have some sleepless nights. I assume that it's due to a combination of a break in routine, lack of mental stimulation, or exhaustion from spending the term coping with school. Sometimes it may be the result of grandparents spoiling her with too many sugary treats. While I believe that diet may contribute to changing moods and undesirable behavior, it is not always the culprit. Some children are very sensitive to dietary issues, others hardly react at all. We've had plenty of sleepless nights when nothing unusual has been consumed.

We all know that a break in regular routine often has an unsettling affect, but by the end of term the kids really need that break. After eight to twelve weeks of sensory overload, anxieties, thinking, and learning, their nervous system needs a change of pace. At the same time, maybe the stress and strain they endure all day at school helps their brain to shut off at night and when they are on holidays they don't have the same level of brain-fatigue.

The challenge is to give them the rest and refreshment they need without completely abandoning structure. We try to compensate with a lot of physical activity: visiting parks and play centres and taking walks and bike rides to get them out in the fresh air and give them plenty of fun exercise. We find it hard to motivate the kids to do educational and learning activities at home. Their place of learning has always been where they learn, while home is their safe haven where they can chill out and relax.

We don't have an answer yet, but we are always working on providing enough structure to keep them feeling comfortable, different forms of mental stimulation, plenty of exercise, and as much sleep and alone-time as they need. Usually it only takes a few days for things to settle down.

Chapter Thirty-Two

Surviving an Overseas Holiday

"Connection is what moves this
world forward. Connection is a
profound human experience."

~ JENNY PALMIOTTO

Creating connections with the world around you is one of our biggest challenges, and if you had told me a few years ago that we might even consider taking our kids on an overseas family holiday, I wouldn't have believed you. At that stage, a basic trip down the street was both a mission and a potential nightmare that more often than not ended in tears. It took a very long process to get to this point.

Our overseas trip was the result of persistent, but gradually increasing tolerance for new experiences through regular outings, slowly increasing time frames, experimenting with new locations and working out what it requires to be as prepared as possible. None of these incremental steps seemed particularly significant at the time, but the slow build-up of length of stay and variety of places visited until we could plan whole days out, overnight stays, and holidays interstate. Then we decided to take a leap of faith and booked an overseas trip to Fiji.

We chose this first destination carefully: not too long a plane ride (with late night flights so the kids would sleep), hot weather, and both pool and beach at our doorstep because that fitted with what the children enjoy. My parents also agreed to come with us so we knew we would have extra helping hands and support if needed.

Airports are really challenging because of the crowds, the need to line up, the waiting, and the strict processes. Thankfully all the staff were very helpful and accommodating. We found that if we explain our situation, people do their best to make things as quick, easy, and painless as possible. It definitely helped that we had been on a few short flights before and once we were on the plane the kids seemed quite comfortable and excited.

"Be prepared" is always our motto. Every time we leave our house, even if it's just for a quick errand, we take everything but the kitchen sink. So obviously, when going on an overseas trip, we take all the necessary essentials to comfort or entertain the kids if necessary. Better to be over-prepared, rather than not have the particular item needed to rectify or suppress a public meltdown. We always have our survival back pack on hand with change of clothes, underwear, nappies, wipes, water, favourite snacks, favourite toys, iPad, phone, chargers and money to resolve any potential situation. We take it everywhere: to the beach, to breakfast, to the pool... you just never know what you will need, or when you'll need it.

The kids are quite fussy about food, so we made sure that we had a good supply of their usual snacks and favourite foods as a backstop. We also chose a resort that friends had stayed at recently and returned with a glowing report of their experience.

We knew that it was very family oriented, the staff were lovely, all the essentials were within walking distance, so it sounded like a pretty safe place to try.

It was funny, we even fell into a routine during our short holiday, going from breakfast, to room, to pool, back to room, to the beach, to the room: rinse and repeat. Thomas and Madi were both really happy and comfortable with that and, honestly, we couldn't have wished for much more!

Something we thought might never be possible, in fact, was a huge success and now we are confident enough to try another destination and excited about the possibilities before us.

Chapter Thirty-Three

Battle of the Senses

"Low pitched notes really make me feel like
love might be truly possible. High pitched
notes make me feel like I could go crazy
with pain and sadness. Great rhythms
can make me feel like life is freedom."

~ JEREMY SICILE-KIRA

We tend to take a lot of simple everyday sensory experiences
for granted. For people diagnosed with ASD and other
sensory related conditions, things like brushing teeth or hair,
and putting on socks and shoes can be torture. From a very
young age, Madi showed clear signs of sensory issues, but I
didn't quite understand the significance of them. She would not
keep her hair tied back in a ponytail, wear a headband or put
clips in at all. Cutting fingernails was a distressing experience
for everyone involved.

When the kids were little, it was okay that they were naked all the
time. It was simply funny that Madi loved wearing her dad's t-shirts
everywhere but as she got older and refused to wear anything else
even when she left the house we received lots of comments.

Even after we had got over the sense of judgement we felt when people looked at what our children were (or were not) wearing, important things like personal hygiene were still challenging. It's one thing to let your children go out without shoes, it's another to know that they haven't brushed their teeth.

Slowly, we have learnt how to break these things down into tiny, baby steps, so they can build up their tolerance to each particular issue. We let them observe us, we did things together, we were patient, and we lowered our expectations and stopped judging ourselves on their performance. It was such a struggle, but here are some of the specific things we did.

Hair: - We started with basic brushing, counting the strokes. First to 10, then 20, 30, and so on. Eventually we used the same approach to tying back Madi's hair for 10 seconds, then 20 seconds etc. It was a very slow process, but now I can brush Madi's hair, tie it back before we leave the house for school and she will leave it in all day, until she gets in the car at pick up time.

Clothing: - It's the same with her underwear, socks, shoes, and school dress. Madi puts on her socks and shoes in the carpark before going in to school and I have a change of dress for her to put on as soon as she gets in the car in the car park after school. She has learnt that she has to wear all the appropriate attire and have her hair tied back for school but as soon as it's finished, she's free. That's totally fine with me, it represents tremendous progress and it is way better than a meltdown.

When she was younger there were days when it was freezing cold and Madi would not wear a jumper or pants, no matter what. She will only wear certain friendly materials like cotton, t-shirt type material and nothing with elastic at the wrists or waist. I buy clothes two to four sizes bigger, so nothing feels too tight or restrictive. She wears boy-leg, short type briefs for greater comfort and lives in dresses. If it is really cold outside, she will now wear a jumper and pants to play or ride her bike, but as soon as she is in the door, they're off! I am not strict with her at home, but she knows the rules when we go out or to school.

Teeth: - Brushing teeth on a regular basis has been a nightmare. Baby-steps were our secret to success. We started brushing without toothpaste while counting to 5 and slowly increasing the time. At first, we might only do the front, back, or side. We made up songs and sang them as we worked on it. We recently started using electric toothbrushes which have been a major hit! The kids have randomly picked them up to play with all by themselves. For proper brushing we have used the same counting method, gradually progressing and adding toothpaste and rinsing. We found a very friendly, accommodating dentist who looked in Thomas's mouth in the waiting room because he wouldn't sit in the dentist chair.

Soaps and Perfumes: - When I mentioned to a girlfriend that I wasn't wearing scented deodorants or perfume because of the kids' heightened senses, she asked, "What about hand wash?" I had totally forgotten about that! Since then I've experimented with various calming natural fragrances like lavender for my hand soaps and washing powder. I'm not sure if it has made a difference, but it's worth considering everything and removing as many sources of irritation as possible as well as introducing as many possible avenues to comfort and calm.

Many people with ASD have extremely heightened sensory responses and it can be genuinely painful to be exposed to noise, physical stimuli, and other sensations. It's easy to dismiss them and feel like they 'should' be able to tolerate certain things, but it's important to recognise that these apparently minor issues can be overwhelming.

A lot of parents use weighted blankets, weighted toys, and sound reducing headphones to mitigate their child's responses, but we haven't had a lot of success with them. We have tried headphones on a few occasions, but both kids hate anything touching their head. I think it's one of those 'trial and error' areas that depends on each individual child's particular sensory issues and preferences. What doesn't work for one, might be the perfect solution for another... and this is an additional reason to attend seminars, read books, talk to other parents, and participate in online support groups and forums: you never know when you will find a great solution that works for your child.

Chapter Thirty-Four

Coping with Anxiety

"Since understanding and accommodation are outside of our locus of control, we can focus on our own coping mechanisms. This allows us to experience and process much more information and see patterns before others."

~ JOE BIEL

What is Anxiety?

- *"A feeling of worry, nervousness, or unease about something with uncertain outcome."*
- *"A nervous disorder marked by excessive uneasiness and apprehension, typically with compulsive behavior or panic attacks."*
- *"Strong desire or concern to do something to happen."*
- *"People with anxiety disorders frequently have intense, excessive and persistent worry and fear about everyday situations. Often, anxiety disorders involve repeated episodes of sudden feelings of intense anxiety and fear or terror that reach a peak within minutes (panic attacks"*
- *"Noun, plural Anxieties – distress or uneasiness of mind caused by fear of danger or misfortune."*

People with autism often experience high levels of anxiety. It comes in many different forms and varying degrees. Just about anything could be a trigger, especially if the person has heightened sensory awareness, which is very common in children with autism.

Your child may be trying to integrate sensations in their body and may be unsure of what is happening to them. They may not be able to recognise or process their own emotions, or they may be picking up emotional signals from others. They may be feeling overwhelmed by a flood of thoughts, or they may have a sensory overload reaction to lights, clutter, people, or crowds. They may be reacting to change or something new. Any or all of these can trigger intense anxiety in your child and they probably won't be able to identify or communicate the cause verbally.

As parents, we need to be careful that we are not projecting our own anxieties on to our children. They pick up on our emotions very accurately and quickly so it's important that we control our thoughts and genuinely believe in their abilities so that we don't inadvertently create behavioural or communication issues.

It's also our job to try to identify the things that cause their anxiety and try to address it. Keeping a journal can help you identify patterns so that you can predict when it may occur and create strategies to prevent it. I always have an exit strategy in place and am prepared with the relaxation techniques most applicable to my children in case they are needed.

Even though communication is an issue, I know that my children understand much more than they can communicate to us, so when they are calm, I try to explain in simple terms why they may have felt that way earlier. Reassurance is important, and

I'm always looking for ways to help reduce or prevent the anxiety from occurring and, once I've identified triggers, working over time to build tolerance and understanding.

Don't ever just dismiss or ignore their anxiety, even if it seems irrational. Find the cause and either eliminate it or help them cope with it.

Strategies for Handling Anxiety

Over time, you will learn different strategies to cope with your own and your child's anxieties. Staying calm and positive during crises is important, but this is not always easy. We go as far as attempting to reduce or even prevent the anxieties from occurring, as much as possible because when they are anxious, a tantrum or some visible sign of stress often occurs.

"Pick up the paper," will always be more effective than,
"Stop throwing paper."

My son Thomas is a super-sensitive soul. He gets extremely emotional if we raise our voice or use the word, "No." I have found that eliminating 'no' as far as possible and avoiding 'no' situations makes our life much easier, and I'm always looking for alternate language or reasoning that are more effective. This takes self-control on my part as I work on not yelling or instantly reacting with a negative response or tone of voice. My goal is to wait until I can respond in a way that will benefit everyone involved.

I really try to put a positive spin on things and even explain what they could have done differently. As I look for things that I can praise (even if it's just a small part of the task, or something completely different) we both take our focus off the 'problem' and defuse the emotion, so that when we come back to it, we can keep our perspective.

A few of the techniques we have all learned to use include:

- Soothing scratches
- Meditation music
- Deep breaths in and out
- Counting to 10
- Essential oils
- Bath salts
- Sensory relief objects
- Trampoline
- Sensory swing
- Exit strategies and general preparedness.

We've worked hard to discover the best calming influence for each of us (parents as well as children) whether that is: time out, energy outlet or a happy place to release and relax is important. Thomas finds comfort in holding things in his hands and if he wants to carry paper, toys or wear a bit of a dress up to school to help him feel more comfortable, so be it. Madi finds release when she's by herself and we all understand that when she walks away, she wants to be left alone.

Chapter Thirty-Five

Stimming or Self-Stimulatory Behaviour

"Self-stimulatory behavior, also known as stimming, is the repetition of physical movements, sounds or, movement of objects, and is common in individuals with autism. 'Stimming' or 'stims', may include hand flapping, rocking, repeating noises or words, snapping fingers, spinning objects, jumping, among many others. It is often used as a way to calm, stimulate, or express thoughts and feelings."

~ NATIONAL AUTISM ASSOCIATION

Both kids at different times have gone through phases of stimming behaviour which still pops up from time to time. They have lined up different toys and objects quite obsessively. Madi still enjoys jumping up and down on a bed and she tends to rock back and forth quite regularly in the car or at school when she needs to calm herself or is struggling to express something.

A lot of her stimming behavior has been in the middle of the night. She will wake us up by jumping up and down in her bed, squealing, singing, giggling, or repeating different noises for hours on end. For a long time, she had a major obsession with swinging on a swing. I didn't initially understand the extent of her obsession, or the relief it brought her then, but now I do.

She would play with everybody's ears, rubbing our earlobes for hours, even reaching over to touch mine while I was driving. She also went through a really annoying phase of chewing paper, would occasionally spin in circles, for extended periods and she has only just recently stopped sucking her thumb.

In the beginning we tried to stop the stimming behaviors. Some of these behaviors were really annoying, but now that I understand how necessary and important these behaviours were for her to either release energy, process feelings, or calm herself I have learned to become more accepting and patient when these situations occur.

That is part of parenting a child with autism. You learn to understand what is going on inside their head and then try to find ways of managing it. We have tried to find appropriate tools and options for them to use like exercise balls to sit and bounce on, trampolines, swings, finger spinners etc. which can all be important tools that help them to self-regulate their emotions.

More often than not, there is probably an underlying issue or logical reason for your child's behaviour. With time, more knowledge and observation you can make your own assumptions and conclusions and address the issue either to prevent it from occurring or by knowing how to deal with it in the best possible manner.

Controlling Distraction and Impulse

Sometimes it is hard to bring your child out of their zoned-out world and at times they might need to have that time out. They may be getting distracted by all the different noises their 'superman' super-sonic hearing can detect or they may be attempting to process their sensory stimuli.

We learned through ABA to use different techniques to attempt to bring back their attention by redirecting that distraction, getting them to model a repetitive action such as clapping hands, standing up, jumping, touching their head, knocking on a table… basically following an instruction with more than likely some sort of physical, moving element. Once you have bought their attention back, you can then try to ask a question for a response. You may need to repeat this technique a few times in a row.

If they are really excited and energetic, we have learned that it is a great idea to exert that energy by doing something really physical: a walk or ride, a quick jump on a trampoline or a swing. Bubbles are another great solution. Everyone loves bubbles: blowing them, chasing them. They have a magical quality that is perfect for calming, controlling distractions and regaining positive focus.

Creating a Secure Environment

We have really tried to create a safe haven at home and provide our children with spaces where they can feel comfortable and free to be themselves and release their energy whenever they need to. We're lucky that we have the space and resources to do this in our home and I do realise that it's not possible for everyone to accomplish.

We have a trampoline, swing, and large back yard for Thomas to play outdoors because that is what he loves to do. We even put in a pool and spa because of the kids' profound love for water and its amazing relaxation effects. Madi has a comfy couch in a quiet room to chill on when she wants to be alone. We have also set up an indoor sensory swing, a little exercise trampoline, and an exercise ball for sensory stimulation. There is not too much clutter in the house, and they can lie in bed and watch a movie to chill out.

At school, they have the support and understanding of all their teachers, aides, and therapists. They love spending relaxing fun times going to the beach, park and on long walks and visiting grandparents. They know that they are being looked after, have a pretty good, happy life and that they are seriously loved.

Chapter Thirty-Six

Overcoming Isolation

"I love my child, autism and all. But damn, sometimes this is hard."

~ DECIPHERING MORGAN

There was a long period of time where I didn't want to leave the house for fear of being judged, public meltdowns, or my own emotional break down. Home was our safe haven where we could all escape somehow.

Getting the right support and help from friends, family, and therapists was an integral part of overcoming those anxieties. Talking to friend over the phone, usually after a few drinks, helped me to talk through a lot of my emotions. Having family and friends become more aware and understanding of our family needs made a difference. Being prepared and having the necessary items in place for coping and prevention definitely gave us more confidence when heading out and about.

We would try smaller trips without high expectations to places that were less stressful like quiet bush walks or smaller, remote parks where we were less likely to encounter triggers or people that might precipitate a scene.

Inviting people to our house was a lot easier than going out and obviously our kids were more comfortable there. We could eventually go to good friends' houses for a goal orientated period of time and then places where there was at least a kids' play area to entertain them, and then later, as long as we had our survival back pack we could go anywhere and everywhere.

Why do People Respond so Fearfully?

One of the reasons that I tended to stay at home and isolate myself was the fear of judgement when my kids misbehaved. I often received evidence that people assumed that my child's problems were the results of poor parenting and that by giving me some parenting advice I might manage them better.

I later realized that there was also a measure of fear in people's response. The general public don't always respond positively because they are uneducated about the effects of autism and other related conditions. Some may be fearful due to all the misconceptions and myths associated with labels and diagnosis and may not realize that every individual child is different or understand that a label or diagnosis does not completely define a person.

'Should' is Fatal

I suppose that society has always been judgemental and that anyone who chose not to conform has always had to pay a price. But living up to society's rules and expectations can be mentally challenging, damaging, and completely unrealistic. Who sets these standards?

It took us a while to realise that we are the bosses of our own family. That means that if we choose to do things a certain way, that's OK. I have come to the realisation that basically whatever works for our family, within reason and with exceptions, is just fine.

After all:

- Who says you have to wear shoes?
- Who says kids have to be bathed, fed and in bed by 7pm?
- Who says when your child should speak and what they should be saying?

Attempting to live up to all human unwritten rules and standards is simply unrealistic for some and has a really negative affect on your whole family. Every person is different, and every family is different too.

Chapter Thirty-Seven

Developing Speech and Conversational Skills

"Vibrant waves of sequenced patterns
emerged in my head whenever I looked at
musical notes and scores. Like pieces of
a mysterious puzzle solved, it was natural
for me to see music and its many facets as
pictures in my head. It never occurred to
me that others couldn't see what I saw."

~ DR STEPHEN SHORE

Our Speech Therapy Journey

When Madi was first diagnosed, speech therapy did not have any sort of impact because she couldn't follow instructions. Through ABA we started working on really basic skills like being able to sit at a table and follow a task or instruction before we returned to a focus on speech. Because most children learn to speak naturally, we don't think about how many steps precede the utterance of meaningful sounds.

Once we started focusing on their speech we went right back to basics. First, it was working on moving the mouth, then modelling and helping them to mimic different sounds. We went step by step until eventually "mmmm" became "mum". This took weeks or months of therapy, and it is still the absolute best word in the world and I still love to hear it every single time they say it!

At one workshop they suggested encouraging your kids to drink through a crazy straw and blow bubbles into it to help develop their facial muscles and assist with speech.

Now at ages 9 and 7, with the help of our NDIS funding, both kids have started speech and ABA therapy again. They are in a completely different stage of development since they have that basic speech, understanding and compliance to help them succeed and meet each lesson's challenge.

Persistence and Repetition

We continued to speak to the kids using regular day-to-day conversation, even when they were not responding at all. We would say "Good morning," every morning, "Hello," and wave during the day, "Goodnight," every night. As their speech started to develop we would prompt their responses, "Say good morning, Mum". Over time they would then begin to copy that response. Gradually they would respond without the prompt. It took years, but one morning, Madi initiated the conversation with a totally unprompted, "Good morning, Mum"!

Working on speech and conversational skills has been a very slow and long process and is still a work in progress. Saying one word, then putting two words together, then three words, and finally, a complete sentence. Making requests, recognising letters, words, people, names, objects etc. Wow! Everything had to be taught in tiny baby steps over time.

The kids were taught eventually at ABA to use "I want…" to request something. Now that their speech has progressed, one of our first targets back is to update that to, "Can I please have…"

It's funny because Madi still doesn't willingly speak most of the time. She can recite the alphabet, sing songs, quote movies and read, but she still can't hold a flowing conversation. Thomas is now starting to come out with a lot of unprompted speech, comments and questions which is awesome! Every time our kids say something, especially something new, my husband and I look lovingly at each other in sheer disbelief, because it's so surreal.

A few weeks ago, after an hour-long car ride home from my parent's house during which Thomas did not stop talking or asking questions for the whole time I actually thought to myself, "This is what people were talking about, this is what it was meant to be like!" Someone asked me then whether I told him to shut up, (LOL!). I will never, ever ask them not to speak after praying for so long that they would find words!

Dealing with Frustration (in Communication and in General)

It was extremely mentally challenging when both kids were effectively non-verbal. Talking to the kids was like talking to a brick wall and extremely frustrating. I even choreographed a dance to the song called, "Say something…" There were times again where it all seemed too hard, but we never gave up!

It is really hard for everyone involved, children and parents, to remain patient, focused and enthusiastic especially when you are not seeing any progress or development. The pressure of feeling as though you are a failure as a parent begins to compound and you just can't understand why your child is unable to learn. Trying to remain patient and using repetitive techniques are really important at this time of frustration, and it's another reason why iPads and other inanimate tutors are so helpful.

Taking a break and trying again at another time or another day is ok. It really doesn't help if either or both of you are getting really upset and frustrated. Getting to know how far you can push your child and judging when they need to have a break is very important. If you are both getting frustrated that you are not achieving a certain goal or task, move on to something else. You can always revisit it at another stage.

Chapter Thirty-Eight

Communications Skills... of All Sorts

"Silence is golden... unless you have
a non-verbal child with Autism."

~ MONIQUE CAIN

Inside the Mind of an Autistic Child

One day I hope that my children will be able to tell me exactly
what is going on in their beautiful minds but for now I can
only imagine and assume what is happening.

They are both now able to recognise certain emotions, but
we are presently working with their therapists so that they can
verbally express why they are feeling a certain way or what has
triggered a particular emotion. I am constantly judging their
behavior and reactions by what I have read, learned and observed,
following their cues as much as possible.

From these observations I can guess the intensities they endure
on a daily basis and try to make them as comfortable as I can. I can

see that the external onslaught is quite chaotic at times, making it hard to relax, and to process their overactive thoughts and feelings. ASD kids are usually not very good at multitasking and find it hard to deal with a lot of thoughts at the same time.

Helping Your Child Connect and Build Relationships

Spending regular, quality time with your child is really important to help you connect and build a positive relationship with them. You need to explore and find out what their passions are, so that you can encourage them to do things they enjoy and share those moments together. This will help your child realise that relationships are a mixture of work and fun.

If your child doesn't learn how to build relationships within the family, it's even harder for them to relate to people outside. We've found it important to keep regular quality family time in our schedule no matter how busy we are. This might include reading to them every night or going to the skate park together once a week. Whatever you do, it is important to maintain that regular connection. We have now progressed from just our family weekend skate park trips at the local skate park to visiting lots of different skate parks and taking our best friends' kids along too!

Starting at home will open doors into the wider world. Follow your child's passions and encourage the things they love to do. It was Madi's love of dancing at home that drove me to keep exploring different dance classes. I kept paints on hand so we could all have regular painting sessions together, with Thomas's love of paper and flying things we started building kites and then going out to fly them together.

147

I was constantly working on ways of entering into their world and incorporating some kind of exchange to give them ideas and guidelines for relating with others. Whether it is playing side by side on the floor, lining up toys next to theirs or playing with whatever strange thing they are into at the time I tried to remain aware and keep looking for different ways of engaging them.

When they have some hobbies and passion, finding other like-minded people to associate with helps build connections, without requiring a lot of verbal interaction. Over time, other people learn to see when they may need some space and the shared interest helps them look beyond the need for a response.

Madi has always loved water and been able to spend hours on end entertained and relaxed by it. Recently, with her dad's excited encouragement, she has taken up surfing! It's one of those activities that doesn't require real conversation or interaction with others but, like skating, can include them. Hopefully, this will be a long-term love and activity they can do together. We thought initially that wearing a wetsuit when necessary might be an issue, but it hasn't been a problem at all. She will often verbally request 'surf board'! Over a period of about two years, she has progressed to learning to paddle a bit herself and, when pushed onto a wave, can stand up and balance from the full lying down position! We will definitely pursue this. It also helps that we all love going to the beach, so it's something that we can all enjoy as a family. The other day, she was literally in the water surfing for two-and-a-half hours straight and other friends with their kids were there too! It's safe to say that she loves it!

Chapter Thirty-Nine

Practicing / Developing Communication Skills

"You don't have to have autism
to notice every detail...
Your child is telling you something
with everything you do.
Are you listening?"

~ STUART DUNCAN

It was really hard to try to connect and communicate with both kids when they were little. We had to learn, try and persist with all different and new ways of connection and communication. ABA provided us with the key we needed to break things down into tiny steps and to break tension when needed and I'd like to share our experience, and some of the things that worked for us.

At first, asking them to follow a simple instruction or answer a question was like talking to a brick wall. We had to keep persisting, continuing to talk even when we didn't receive any response, replying to our own questions. Modelling, modelling, modelling and using short, simple sentences.

We would sing songs with actions and made up our own songs relating to everyday living as we were driving in the car, jumping on the trampoline, or standing there pushing a swing. Anytime there was an opportunity, especially in a happy environment for the kids, we would sing the alphabet song. Singing, "I Can Sing a Rainbow" and many different educational songs became a bedtime routine. Encouraging and teaching them to follow actions and imitate other people is a really vital step in getting them to follow further instructions.

We knew that the kids loved watching movies, over and over again. So, we would watch with them attempting to engage in conversation like asking them questions about the movie and different characters, or even getting them to repeat dialogue from the movie.

We've used the iPad communication apps to teach all sorts of things, as well as to film ourselves modelling actions, using language, and acting out different social scenarios for our children to watch and copy.

Repetition of words and requests helps the kids to process it properly the first time and, if they are really having difficulty or need to concentrate, ensuring that your environment is quiet and distraction-free is essential. Once the kids were speaking themselves, we would repeat their words back to them. We really made a point of praising them, using fun, positive reinforcement or rewards, to encourage that positive behavior.

Visual cues can be really helpful especially for the kids that have difficulties in verbal communication. A lot of people have suggested learning sign language as another form of communication which takes the pressure off them when they are under stress because it doesn't require as many different senses as speaking and listening. In a way, we have developed our own form of sign language using descriptive actions. There are lots of different creative ways to communicate and interact, it just takes some openness and ingenuity to find them.

Chapter Forty

Finding Balance

"Your whole life can't be one
big therapy session."

~ MEGAN INGRAM

Trying to find a healthy balance in our lives has been really difficult. Your life does become consumed by your children and their needs. We were desperately trying everything we could to help them. We were dealing with our own emotions and grief. We were consumed by guilt when we even thought about doing something for ourselves.

The kid's original speech therapist said to me, "Your whole life can't be one big therapy session." That has really resonated with me because that is certainly how it has felt most of the time.

You're always adjusting your way of life, what you do, how you speak, and working everything around what you can and can't manage. You feel guilty when you are not doing something to help your kids and feel like you should always be doing more. You also feel bad if you just need to have a rest!

I have tried to keep up with regular work and exercise, despite the guilt. In the end you don't do anyone any favours if you let the stress and tension build up. An hour or two escaping, releasing endorphins and focusing on something other than your kids makes you feel like a person, rather than just a special needs parent, but you need help and support to be able to do that.

Let People Know What Your Life is Really Like

If people are completely unaware of how your children are fully affected, how you are feeling, or how it has all compounded to affect every part of your life, how can others truly support you? I know some people are not comfortable with exposing or sharing their deepest, darkest secrets, feelings or disclosing a diagnosis but personally I have found that shedding more light on your situation can have a very positive affect all round.

For me, this was partly a pride issue. It meant acknowledging that things weren't perfect… that I wasn't perfect. But, once I opened up, I found help, support, and encouragement in some unexpected places and forms. If people know what you're going through, they can be more empathetic. If they don't fully understand, they can't be the friend or support that you truly need.

Your Child is Affected by Your Mood and Energy

Judging by my personal experience, I truly believe that my emotions, reactions, mental state, approach and general mood affects that of my children. This means that your children's progress and well-being can be directly influenced by your choices to exercise, take break and have some fun, do whatever it takes to truly energise you and lift your mood.

Trust me... kids with autism are quick to sense what is really going on inside you. Make that positive, can do attitude a reality. Also, be careful not to push your own fears or insecurities on to your children. They may be coping, but their anxieties may increase if they can sense that stress or insecurity in you.

You really do need to start thinking differently and consider taking a different approach to your daily life. Maybe you need to adjust what you do and how you speak. You probably need to be open to accepting help from a lot of other people. And you'll certainly need to think outside the box and explore different ways of teaching and learning, like singing instead of reading a book.

You can define your own measures of peace and happiness that can really transform the way you think and your approach to life. As you make a habit of gauging, observing, thinking... and only then reacting in a positive and calm manner you'll notice things change.

Things You Can Do to Control Chaos and Make Life Easier

- Most days I try to get up early, before the kids, at 5:30 or 6am, to do some exercise so that I have done at least one thing healthy for myself each day, especially if I may not get a chance later on.
- I try to be really organized to counter all the chaotic possibilities.
- I have clothes out ready for everyone for the next day before I go to bed the night before.

- I have the kids' lunch's or snacks (as much as possible) packed the night before ready to go.
- I may cook three meals at once, for the whole week, to give myself and the kids more time other nights.
- Our survival back pack is always packed by the front door, ready to just grab as I run out the door and I always have one in the car as a backup, just in case.

Finding that balance for your children is also important. Their life can't be one whole therapy session either! No matter how much they need to learn, they also need to have plenty of down time, where they can chill out, relax and not be hounded to learn, contend with social or sensory stimuli, or speak.

We tried to work out a schedule that gave them a variety of different therapies and classes as well as alternating between one-on-one, small group, and larger class sizes to expose the kids to all different scenarios. Their week days have been jam-packed with activity, so weekends we try to focus on outdoor activities and visiting grandparents' houses... all the things they love to do!

Chapter Forty-One

Who Are Your Supporters?

"All it takes is a beautiful fake smile to hide an injured soul and they will never notice how broken you really are."

~ ROBIN WILLIAMS

I know I've mentioned this before, but it's crucial to your survival. You need a support team... people who know that your soul is injured and who you let inside.

For us, our parents became our best friends. Apart from our own home, their houses were the safe haven for ourselves and our children. My cousin, who is more like my sister, and her partner, have been our other really trusted support. It helped that she truly loves kids and is qualified in that field, including experience working with kids with additional needs. So, she was more than simply qualified and understanding, she also loves the kids like they were her own family.

I know that not all of you will have that kind of family support, but I want to urge you to look around for people who could care like that and to be ready to open up and express your need for support and assistance. Maybe it will be your friends, or maybe church, other parents with special needs' kids. I do know that you will be grateful for every helping hand along the way and that they will be there, if you look.

All of our ABA team, staff, therapists, and other families involved at the centre provided seriously important support and we certainly would not be here today without them. They helped and guided us through our toughest time and not only helped our kids but taught us how we could connect and communicate with them.

Now all of our school aides are our guardian angles and like family. They are like second mums, who support us every day of the week, assisting our children to learn and grow academically, socially, and in every area of life. They are so caring and truly invested and they can encourage our kids to do more than we can in so many ways so we can go to work with complete confidence and peace of mind that they are in the best care.

My dance teacher and everyone involved with my happy place, have been a major constant escape, love and support. She encouraged and helped me to continue with an alternate, creative passion and guided me through some of my darkest days. After starting the children's all abilities dance class initially for Madi, she now also teaches an adult all-abilities weekly class too. Some people just have that special aura and beautiful soul that can connect and make a real difference and impact on people's lives. My spiritual mother also kept pursuing a relationship with my daughter Madi and all our love of dance and I could not be more thankful. She persisted, encouraged and accommodated us and now they too share a special bond and relationship with each other, opening and exploring a whole new world together.

Without a doubt, my counsellor also played a major part in my survival and revival and was a key support in my deepest and darkest time of need. Just look at what her clarity and encouragement of writing has enabled me to create from my thoughts and feelings.

Last but not least, our friends, both old and new. We are so incredibly grateful to all of our beautiful besties that have staunchly supported us our whole adult lives. Through thick and thin, the good, the bad and the ugly. We have always known they were there for us, whenever we needed them to be a shoulder to cry on, a support to lean on, and an encouragement to have fun again. We have also made many new friends along the way, friends who have shared our autism journey.

We have been truly blessed to have crossed paths with so many amazing people and we could not be more grateful. You need a support team too. And you'll find them if you look around.

So, who are they?

Chapter Forty-Two

Survive and Thrive: You and Your Children

"Our experiences are all unique.
Regardless, I do believe that it is
important to find the beautiful. Recognise
that there is bad, there is ugly, there
is disrespect, there is ignorance and
there are meltdowns. Those things are
inevitable. But there is also good."

~ ERIN MCKINNEY

After ten years, we are just at the start of our journey with autism. There is so much to learn, so much to trial, so much to experience. In the midst of apparent failure, frustration, and suffering I've learned that there are many good and beautiful moments that flash across, even in the midst of our hardest struggles. They're easy to miss, though, especially if I'm focused on making judgements and comparisons.

If there is one message that I want to share with other parents of children with autism, it's the message of hope. You really never know what will happen. I'm not ignoring the fact that quite probably neither Madi nor Thomas will ever be able to live alone and fully support themselves and my husband and I have made provision for that possibility... but we don't know!

The world and our society **are** changing... and that change brings hope for every 'misfit'. It's our role as parents to help our children develop the talents and strengths they have been given and to love them unconditionally. It's not our place to shut them away and pretend they have nothing to offer.

This is not the direction I imagined my life would take, but I've learned so much about myself and others that I might not have learned in any other way. Patience, acceptance, perseverance, self-control... and the need to deal with my own inner demons, so that my beloved children can be set free to deal with theirs. Perhaps it takes having a child who is so sensitive to the energies around them that they pick up on the emotions I think are buried deep inside and act them out to show us the importance of our own emotional integrity. I know that was the inspiration for my determination to:

Do Whatever it Takes, and Never, Never, Give Up on Loving My Autistic Children and Helping Them Flourish!

May you also find the resources, strength, and support you need to love and serve your own autistic children. I hope this book will encourage you on your journey.

~ Monique Cain.

Chapter Forty-Three

Acknowledgements

"Wanting to be free. Wanting to
be me. Trying to make people see.
And accept the real me."

~ Scott Lentine

There are so many people who have helped us in our journey, that I can only name a few of them. If I haven't mentioned you by name here, please don't feel offended or overlooked, know that I have named you in my heart. As I mentioned in an earlier chapter, the quality and extent of your support network is intensely important for every family who deals with autism.

I'd like to express my intense appreciation to: -

- Nicole & John Devine for their initial support after diagnosis and guiding us towards Abacus Learning Centre and ABA.
- Dimitra Arthur, our Child Psychologist at Sprout, for guiding us through all our diagnosis processes and report-writing needs.
- Megan Ingram, from Peninsula Speech, for being so kind and helpful especially around the initial diagnosis stages.

- The staff, therapists, and associated families at Abacus Learning Centre, especially Lauren, Nina, Emma, Kathryn and Jody who have supported us form the very beginning. You completely changed our world. You gave us tools, hope, and guidance through our darkest days and are a constant support.
- Biala Mornington, for providing group therapy sessions, counselling and extra kinder support, especially Leanne De Groot.
- Waterfall Gully Kinder, in particular Claire, who was accepting of both our kids, provided outside encouragement as well as the very first reading of 'Madi At Kinder', the first book in The Everyday Autism Series.
- The staff at Little Grasshoppers Day Care Centre, particularly Kaye Ellis.
- Kate, from Peppertree Counselling, for putting me back together when I was broken and encouraging me to write more. I am so proud to have been part inspiration for her own publishing journey of the children's book, "Feelings in my Suitcase"
- Boneo Primary School and all the brilliant teachers and aides (especially Jan, Paula, Sheila, Deb and Mandy) who have been so accepting, inclusive, and helpful as our children learn and grow. For also allowing extra support from The Light Up Autism Foundation with the introduction of ABA sessions in school. Special thanks to Bianca and Marae.
- Barefoot Therapists, particularly Kara, our new speech therapist, and other therapies/groups moving forward.

- Sheron, my dance teacher at Stage Door Dance Academy, for inspiring me to always follow my dreams and providing me with a safe haven, a creative outlet, and her constant role as confidante and support as well as her understanding, perseverance, and love for Madi. She has never given up on her!
- My cousin Gemma, who has always been my sister, best friend, and inspiration. She is the primary influence behind our decision to have another child who became Thomas.
- Sarah, Lin and my editor Debra Hilton for assisting me to create and bring to life, "The Everyday Autism Series" and helping to make my writing dream a reality.
- Andrew Louis who created the sensational illustrations and uncanny cartoon character versions of Madi & Thomas that help to tell our stories pictorially!
- Our Cain & Co family/work colleagues, thank you for always putting up with our craziness and constant mood swings.
- Isla, Madi's best friend, for showing us and Madi that true friendship can be a reality and that kids can see past appearances! Thank you for loving, caring & appreciating her for who she is.
- All of our remarkable friendships with our beautiful best friends, you know who you are... We feel so blessed and thankful to have your undying lifelong love and support!
- Our parents... What can I say! You have lived this journey with us, loved us, suffered with us, supported us, rejoiced with us and our children every step of the way. We could not have done it without you!
- Michael, Madi, and Thomas, you are my whole world and mean everything to me. I have been blessed to experience

absolute true love on so many levels, all the highs and lows. I love you all more than words can express. I would not have achieved half the things I have without you. You are my driving force and my absolute inspiration. I try to be the best person, mother and wife I can be and hope that you are proud of me, too.

- Every single person that has ever been kind, understanding and non-judgmental and helped us along the way (there have been so, so many), THANK YOU!!!

About the Author

Monique Cain

I am married to my high school sweetheart, Michael, and the mother of two very special children: Madi and Thomas. We live in a small seaside town not far from where we both grew up. Michael and I both love outdoor adventures, people, and sports. When we got married, we had our life mapped out and we just knew that our several children would share Michael's love for sport, and mine for dance. It hasn't quite worked out that way, though!

Every parent knows that their children are special ... but ours really are! They are both beautiful, and they are both autistic and they have both taught us important lessons about life and love.

Like most first time parents we were awed and entranced by our baby daughter and we watched with joy as she learned how to walk and started to talk and play with us. Suddenly, when Madi was nearly two years old everything changed. Almost overnight, it seemed, she withdrew, she became fussy about her food and the clothes she would wear, and our sunny, delightful, picture-perfect daughter became a major challenge and we didn't know what was going on.

Soon after Thomas was born, she was diagnosed with Autism Spectrum Disorder (ASD) and our whole life changed as our days were consumed with therapy and appointments. We were assured that there was every chance he would not suffer from ASD, but we were far more conscious of the early-warning signs for him, so when we started to feel uneasy we had him tested.

With two children with autism, and a part-time job, my life became a whirl of appointments, tantrums, frustration, embarrassment, and increasing isolation. My kids looked completely normal and every time we ventured out and something upset them I would see and hear people passing judgement on me as a parent. From the outside, I seemed to be coping, but inside I was a total mess!

Thanks to my supportive husband, both our families, our children's dedicated therapists, and a wise counsellor who taught me to acknowledge and respect how I truly felt and encouraged me to write about my journey, I have slowly journeyed forward to a place where I feel I can reach out to others and share both the highs and lows of my journey in the hopes of encouraging others.

My journey as an author began with simple rhyming stories the teacher read aloud to help Madi's kinder class understand her better. The original book became a series which has helped to raise awareness about autism in general and teach both adults and children how to interact with children with autism. As I speak and am interviewed I receive a lot of questions about life with two autistic children, and I recognise the pain, self-judgement, and guilt that I experienced myself. It is my hope to continue to share my journey as encouragement and affirmation for other parents of autistic children, and as insight for their family and friends.

I regularly speak at events and seminars on autism.

For more information visit my speaker page:
https://theeverydayautismseries.com.au/speaker

or contact me via LinkedIn:
https://www.linkedin.com/in/monique-cain

For More Resources and Support on coping with autism and educating friends and family head to:

TheEverydayAutismSeries.com.au/resources

For regular inspiration and encouragement or to learn more about our autism journey go to:

Facebook.com/theeverydayautismseries
Instagram.com/theeverydayautismseries

To purchase *The Everyday Autism Series* picture books go to:

TheEverydayAutismSeries.com.au/books

www.ingramcontent.com/pod-product-compliance
Lightning Source LLC
Chambersburg PA
CBHW021402090426
42742CB00009B/972